Shakespeare in the Theatre: Cheek by Jowl

Shakespeare in the Theatre: Cheek by Jowl

Peter Kirwan

THE ARDEN SHAKESPEARE

LONDON • NEW YORK • OXFORD • NEW DELHI • SYDNEY

THE ARDEN SHAKESPEARE
Bloomsbury Publishing Plc
50 Bedford Square, London, WC1B 3DP, UK
1385 Broadway, New York, NY 10018, USA

BLOOMSBURY, THE ARDEN SHAKESPEARE and the Arden Shakespeare logo are
trademarks of Bloomsbury Publishing Plc

First published in Great Britain 2019
This paperback edition published 2020

A catalogue record for this book is available from the British Library.

Library of Congress Cataloging-in-Publication Data
Names: Kirwan, Peter, author.
Title: Cheek by Jowl / Peter Kirwan.
Description: London, UK ; New York, NY : The Arden Shakespeare, 2019. |
Series: Shakespeare in the theatre | Includes bibliographical references
and index.
Identifiers: LCCN 2018055823| ISBN 9781474223294 (hardback) | ISBN
9781474223317 (ePDF) | ISBN 9781474223300 (eBook)
Subjects: LCSH: Cheek by Jowl (Theater group) | Theatrical
companies–England–London. | Shakespeare, William, 1564-1616–Stage
history–1950-
Classification: LCC PN2596.L7 C225 2019 | DDC 792.09421–dc23
LC record available at https://lccn.loc.gov/2018055823

ISBN: HB: 978-1-4742-2329-4
         PB: 978-1-4742-2328-7
         ePDF: 978-1-4742-2331-7
         eBook: 978-1-4742-2330-0

Series: Shakespeare in the Theatre

Typeset by Integra Software Services Pvt. Ltd.
Printed and bound in Great Britain

To find out more about our authors and books visit www.bloomsbury.com and sign up
for our newsletters.

CONTENTS

FIGURES

SERIES PREFACE

Each volume in the *Shakespeare in the Theatre* series focuses on a director or theatre company who has made a significant contribution to Shakespeare production, identifying the artistic and political/social contexts of their work.

The series introduces readers to the work of significant theatre directors and companies whose Shakespeare productions have been transformative in our understanding of his plays in performance. Each volume examines a single figure or company, considering their key productions, rehearsal approaches and their work with other artists (actors, designers, composers). A particular feature of each book is its exploration of the contexts within which these theatre artists have made their Shakespeare productions work. Thus, the series not only considers the ways in which directors and companies produce Shakespeare, but also reflects upon their other theatre activities and the broader artistic, cultural and socio-political milieu within which their Shakespeare performances and productions have been created. The key to the series' originality, then, is its consideration of Shakespeare production in a range of artistic and broader contexts; in this sense, it de-centres Shakespeare from within Shakespeare studies, pointing to the range of people, artistic practices and cultural phenomena that combine to make meaning in the theatre.

Series editors:
Peter Holland, Farah Karim-Cooper and Stephen Purcell

ACKNOWLEDGEMENTS

I fell in love with Cheek by Jowl's work in 2004 when Carol Chillington Rutter took my undergraduate class to see *Othello* at Riverside Studios, a life-changing experience that led me to make writing about theatre my life's work. The opportunity to write a book about Cheek by Jowl is one I never imagined getting, and I'm grateful to the series editors for inviting me to contribute to this series.

My greatest debt is to Declan Donnellan and Nick Ormerod, who have been extraordinarily generous with their time, as well as allowing me to attend rehearsals for *The Winter's Tale* and inviting me to join the company in Moscow and Paris. This book could not have been written without their openness, and I hope that the book does justice to their life's work. Thank you, too, for the work that has transformed my own and so many others' understanding of Shakespeare and his contemporaries.

The Cheek by Jowl team have been welcoming (and patient!). Thank you to Beth, Caroline, Eleanor, Marie, Sarah, Simone and Teya for their practical help – especially Simone for wrangling the Russian visa – and insights. I want to especially acknowledge Dominic Kennedy, the company's archivist, whose support throughout has gone above and beyond. Dominic's work on the Sophie Hamilton Archive has cemented the company's legacy, and this book is indebted to his work and unwavering cheerfulness.

The book is deeply informed by the conversations I have had with Cheek by Jowl's alumni. While there wasn't space to include everyone's memories, I want to thank the following for making time to share their experiences: Xavier Boiffier, Beth Byrne, Fausto Cabra, David Collings, Alexander Feklistov,

Jane Gibson, Judith Greenwood, Anastasia Hille, Owen Horsley, Orlando James, Anna Khalilulina, Anya Kolesnikova (who also generously translated for the Russian actors), Jenia Kolesnikova, Eleanor Lang, Adrian Lester, Cécile Leterme, Matthew Macfadyen, Michelangelo Marchese, Barbara Matthews, Peter Moreton, Natalie Radmall-Quirke, Joy Richardson, Marcus Roche, James Shapiro, Arantxa Vela, Timothy Walker and Laura Zangarini. Thanks also to the 2016 *Winter's Tale* company for making me feel so welcome in the rehearsal room.

The School of English at the University of Nottingham granted me a sabbatical and funding support to conduct research. I'm grateful to Lia and Deb, Andy and Jimmy, and especially Justine Williams for putting me up for extended stays. My colleagues in the School of English have been extraordinarily supportive – thanks especially to Jem Bloomfield, Sarah Grandage, Georgie Lucas, Jim Moran, Jo Robinson, Nicola Royan and Lucie Sutherland. A special thanks also to Hannah Manktelow for her speed and accuracy in transcribing interviews, and to Margaret Bartley, Mark Dudgeon, Lara Bateman and the Arden Shakespeare team for their guidance and patience.

I'm grateful to the many colleagues who have given me time and space to talk about Cheek by Jowl. Part of Chapter 1 began as a paper at Queen's University Belfast at the invitation of Edel Lamb and Mark Thornton Burnett, and part of Chapter 2 was originally generated for the 'Offensive Shakespeare' conference organized by Edmund King and Monika Smialkowska at Northumbria University. My general editor, Bridget Escolme, has been supportive throughout, and I've benefitted from conversations with Paul Prescott, Kathryn Prince, Stephen Purcell, Carol Rutter, Robert Shaughnessy and many others. Pascale Aebischer is a wonderful mentor who probably doesn't realize how important her support has been to me, so I'd like to acknowledge publicly here how essential her guidance and encouragement are. Thank you to everyone who has shared their love of the company.

Finally, thank you as always to my amazing family and idiotic cat for their love and support, especially during some difficult patches during the process. Susan Anderson became central to my life just as I began the research, and has been its most tireless supporter. This book is dedicated, with all my love, to her.

Introduction

Who are Cheek by Jowl? The question is perhaps the most obvious with which to begin a book about one of the most acclaimed theatre companies of the last half-century, but as Declan Donnellan sets out in his acting masterclass in book form, *The Actor and the Target*, the search for insight defies not only simple answers but also simple questions.

> Trying to answer '*Who am I?*' is a lifetime's work for the individual, and indeed the more we discover ourselves, the more we realise that we don't know ourselves at all. If, then, we cannot properly answer the question about ourselves, how can we possibly answer it about someone else? (Donnellan 2005: 76)

When the actor asks 'Who am I?' they risk settling for an easy description that will ultimately paralyse them, because any answer that can be so easily distilled is static. Donnellan prefers different questions:

> What questions would help Irina [his hypothetical actor] more? '*Who would I like to be*' is more useful because it implies an answer that moves. '*Who would I like to be?*' is even more useful when asked with a near opposite such as: '*Who am I afraid I might be?*' (Donnellan 2005: 76)

For thirty-five years, Cheek by Jowl has been keeping actors moving by changing the questions. Donnellan's ethos of removing the fear that blocks actors, rather than telling actors what they should do, is married with Nick Ormerod's responsive designs in a 'symbiotic indivisibility' (Prescott 2008: 70) that grows organically around the work of the actor, rather than presenting cages to which the actor is confined. As Ormerod puts it, 'I want to make the actors as free as possible to move. Movement and flow keep the play alive' (2016). At the centre of Cheek by Jowl is an ethos of potential rather than definition.

This study of Cheek by Jowl's work on Shakespeare is the first book-length scholarly study of the company, a project that necessitates some definition of who Cheek by Jowl are. On some levels, this is straightforward. Cheek by Jowl is an acclaimed international touring company, directed by the professional and personal partnership of Donnellan and Ormerod, which presents classical (and occasionally new) plays in three languages.[1] The company began touring productions around the UK on a shoestring budget in 1981, supported by the Arts Council with a grant of £6,000; Cheek by Jowl was a beneficiary of the insight and acumen of Ruth Marks, 'responsible for promoting and championing some of the best of 1980's touring theatre from within the Arts Council' (Reade 1991: 12). Then, with support from the British Council, the company extended its tours across continental Europe and beyond, establishing a reputation for 'the reappraisal of classic texts' (Rutter 2005: 346), usually with a contemporary or timeless setting that made the productions feel like new writing. Cheek by Jowl has toured to over 300 cities across six continents, launched countless careers and begun producing its own Russian and French work.[2] The company has a recognizable and influential style, and in Europe is ranked alongside the great European auteurs.[3] And as the company's name – a quotation from *A Midsummer Night's Dream* – may suggest, Shakespeare is core to its repertoire.

The constant motion of Cheek by Jowl frustrates easy definition, however. The company may have an administrative office at London's Barbican Centre as part of its Artistic Associate status, but the productions are always on the move, often dropping in for a mere handful of performances in any one country, including in recent years the UK. The company is clearly part of the European theatrical establishment – as recently as July 2016, Donnellan was awarded the Golden Lion of Venice for Lifetime Achievement, the latest in a long line of honours and celebrations – and yet the company still prefers mid-sized venues that allow intimacy between audience and company.[4] Several of the company's innovations of its first decade – a commitment to colour-blind casting, productions featuring an all-male company (Chapter 3), the use of actors as musicians, the distinctive practice of overlapping scenes (Chapter 4) – are now common practice in British theatre, making it harder to pin down the elusive Cheek by Jowl style.[5] And artistically the company has refused to settle, with recent productions introducing video projection, live filming and even pre-built sets.

The one constant of Cheek by Jowl is its prime directive: the company exists to serve the artistic work of Donnellan and Ormerod, as perhaps best articulated in a 1991 policy document.

We are a director-led company. The reputation of Cheek by Jowl is intrinsically bound up with that of Declan Donnellan and Nick Ormerod. One of the reasons for their continued success is their attention to detail. Shows are regularly visited, reworked and re-rehearsed on tour; casting is meticulous and takes months; plays are only chosen after weeks of reading and debate … we are determined not to compromise our standards, nor to cease our exploration of increasingly challenging work. (Cheek by Jowl 1991a: 3)

As the minutes of a 1995 board retreat state, 'CbyJ IS Declan and Nick's work,' and the company's board exists to provide a regular fixed framework for this work (Cheek by Jowl 1995a). The relationship between Cheek by Jowl and Donnellan and Ormerod, however, is more of a tight Venn diagram than an exact synonymy. Donnellan and Ormerod have always worked regularly outside of Cheek by Jowl; they have directed classics, new work, musicals, opera and films, and among their more notable extracurricular activities can be found the British premieres of Lope de Vega's *Fuente Ovejuna* (National Theatre, 1989), Tony Kushner's *Angels in America* (National Theatre, 1992 and 1993) and Lee Hall's stage adaptation of *Shakespeare in Love* (Noel Coward Theatre, 2014). For actors who have worked with Donnellan and Ormerod both within and without Cheek by Jowl, such as Joy Richardson and Orlando James, there is no difference in the process (James 2016; Richardson 2016). On the other hand, Cheek by Jowl has on two occasions produced work with other artists at the helm: Calderon's *The Doctor of Honour* (1989) was directed by Lindsay Posner, who had formerly served as assistant director on *The Man of Mode* (1985), and in 1997 long-standing cast member Timothy Walker directed the British premiere of Tennessee Williams's *Out Cry*, with Ormerod designing.

If Cheek by Jowl doesn't exactly equate to Ormerod and Donnellan, however, it is the space in which they work most freely; as the policy document states, 'It is the environment in which their best work is likely to be done and the means by which it can most easily be taken to audiences throughout the country' (Cheek by Jowl 1991a: 3). Ormerod and Donnellan begin rehearsals with a clean slate – they don't present box designs on the first day or tell actors how they will interpret the text. Rather, design and interpretation emerge through the process of rehearsal, meaning that set, costumes, lighting designs and even some roles are decided very late in the process, which can cause a clash of priorities in larger institutions; as Ormerod notes, at the National 'things are required 13 weeks in advance and Declan hates planning things. That works fine with Cheek by Jowl, because we start with a tabula rasa … out of which the best work comes' (Curtis 1994). Actor Fausto

Cabra sees this as the risk-taking that makes the company unique:

> [The] work starts from the human beings who are venturing on a journey on the stage together. Ideas, images, expedients, special effects, breathtaking scenes, the director's intelligent rendition of a play etc. must be subordinate to that starting point ... What Declan and Nick do is, in the highest sense of the term, a theatre of research, since it explores the essence of the theatrical question: how to reproduce life? (Cabra 2018)

Cheek by Jowl is the environment that enables Ormerod and Donnellan to realize their most complete creative process while being supported by a dedicated team sensitive to the requirements of the work and to deliver this to a network of receptive international theatres. In 2005, Cheek by Jowl entered into an innovative residency at the Barbican (then programmed by Louise Jeffreys) to produce three annual seasons pairing an English and a Russian production, for which the Barbican remodelled its main auditorium to allow an audience of only 400 people to sit on the stage, beginning with a double bill of *The Changeling* and *Twelfth Night* (Coveney 2006; Cheek by Jowl 2007c);[6] Les Geméaux in Sceaux is a current favourite for opening tours, with its willingness to go dark long before opening to allow for extended rehearsals on the stage (Horsley 2016). Cheek by Jowl is devoted to the ideal of the tour, creating portable work that will speak to a multilingual audience and to the idea that a production is never 'fixed' (Donnellan 2009: 71).

This book chooses, then, to focus on Cheek by Jowl as a company rather than on Donnellan and Ormerod as individual theatre-makers, and early modern drama is where Cheek by Jowl and Donnellan/Ormerod most consistently overlap (see Appendix). Donnellan has 'an intense relationship with the work of Shakespeare' (Donnellan 2009: 77), and to date the company has presented some twenty-two productions of sixteen early modern plays in English, Russian and French, as well as others outside the Cheek by Jowl framework. Some of these rank among the most canonical of twentieth-century Shakespeare productions, and others have received less discussion. While this book cannot be exhaustive, the case studies selected exemplify the company's approach to the radical reinterpretation of Shakespeare.

The Cheek by Jowl family

At the opening of *Measure for Measure* (2013–), the lights rose on a tightly packed body of individuals standing upstage, all dressed differently: a prisoner, nun, policeman, prostitute, men in suits. They moved downstage, their eyes fixed forward, and paused. They circumnavigated the stage, completing a full loop, then crouched together. They looked up and crossed the stage, staring at the heavens, before stopping and turning to look again at the audience. The group moved on but this time left behind a single suited man still looking at the ceiling. The group completed another circuit and stopped, staring at the lone man, who began walking again before realizing he was alone. He and the group stared at one another from across the stage and reached out their hands towards one another, the group mirroring the man. To the man's apparent discomfort, the group then got onto their knees and began crawling towards him, before moving collectively to bring out a single chair that he reluctantly, slowly sat in. All of this happened in silence.

I will return to this sequence in Chapter 6, but this opening also serves as a metaphor for Cheek by Jowl's work. The production began with a group that moved and functioned as one, but produced individuals from within itself; the group does not forbid individual identity, but the individual's actions are inextricable from their influence on the rest of the ensemble. While Ormerod and Donnellan are the only constants in the

Cheek by Jowl story, their work is characterized by close relationships and long-term collaborations with a large family of contributors.[7] It is testament to the Cheek by Jowl ethos that every member of the UK-based touring company – from the actor playing Hamlet to the assistant stage manager – is paid the same (Cheek by Jowl 1991a: 1). It is worth noting a number of the key players in this history.

Donnellan and Ormerod met at Cambridge University in the 1970s, both studying Law, and their first experience of a European Shakespeare tour was as actors, with Donnellan playing Lennox and Ormerod the Second Murderer in *Macbeth* (Curtis 1994). Ormerod went to design school following graduation, while Donnellan was called to the Bar, and the two worked separately in theatres and odd jobs until 1979 (Reade 1991: 12). The year 1980 saw them collaborate on a fringe production of *'Tis Pity She's a Whore*, but it was an Arts Council grant of £6,000 – applied for under the last-minute name 'Cheek by Jowl' – that allowed the newly founded company's first production, *The Country Wife*, to premiere at the Edinburgh Fringe. With the exceptions noted above, they have directed and designed every Cheek by Jowl production, and apart from a brief hiatus between *Much Ado about Nothing* (1998) and *Homebody/Kabul* (2001–2) – Donnellan and Ormerod needed a break and, as Barbara Matthews says, 'without Nick and Declan, and their work, there was no company' (2016) – they have kept the company in constant production of new work.

Ormerod suggests that 'it's best to work from a permanent team, or as permanent as possible in this changing world' (Donnellan and Ormerod 1996: 85). Cheek by Jowl's official 'Artistic Associates' (Cheek by Jowl 2018a) are its most regular collaborators.[8] These include Paddy Cunneen (music), Jane Gibson (movement), Judith Greenwood (lighting), Owen Horsley (direction), Catherine Jayes (music) and Patsy Rodenburg (voice), but the company enjoys long-standing relationships with several artists, particularly for their Russian and French work. Several of the associates work regularly with Donnellan and Ormerod outside of Cheek by Jowl, and their long-term collaborations have enabled the creative teams to develop a 'common language' (Donnellan and Ormerod 2016) that contributes seamlessly to the Cheek by Jowl style. Regular trusted collaborators have a great deal of creative responsibility – Horsley was asked to give notes in his fourth week as assistant director and was co-director for the recast production of 'Tis Pity She's a Whore in 2012–13 (Horsley 2016); Angie Burns, who has costumed the company since the late 1980s, takes control of fastenings, cut and fitting based on Ormerod's drawings, noting the trust placed in her (Greenwood 1998: 22); Michelangelo Marchese, associate director for Périclès (2018), takes a prominent role in the rehearsal room; and Gibson, who has served as movement director on almost every English- and French-language Cheek by Jowl production since the early 1990s, 'think[s] as a director would think' (Boiffier 2016), her physical work integral to the actors' embodiment. Assistant directors, including Horsley, Marcus Roche and Kirill Sbitnev, often stay with the company across several productions. The artistic influence of long-term contributors such as Cunneen and Greenwood reverberates across the company's work. While these collaborations are key to the company's success, however, freedom is also essential – all of the associates are employed on a freelance basis, meaning that the Cheek by Jowl work is a creative choice for these experienced theatre-makers rather than an obligation.

Equally important to the company's success is the administrative team. Barbara Matthews made up the third of Cheek by Jowl's leading triumvirate from the early 1980s until the end of 'Act One' (Matthews 2016) in 1998. The executive director is responsible for implementing Donnellan and Ormerod's vision in practice, and Matthews' success at this was such that she was able to establish Cheek by Jowl Management Services, formalizing the informal mentoring she was doing for other small businesses (Cheek by Jowl 1991a: 1). The company's archives at the V&A demonstrate the extraordinary complexities of arranging high-profile international tours and generating funding while also preserving the company's distinctive requirements: single rooms for company members, appropriate rest days and other accommodations designed to ensure comfortable working conditions for all (Cheek by Jowl 1995b). Matthews' business acumen had an influence on programming; noting that *Philoctetes* would not support a middle-scale tour by itself, the company paired it with *The Tempest* for the 1988–9 schedule, to enormous success (Matthews 2016). Matthews established the essential framework of the Cheek by Jowl tour that the company's successive executive directors (Roy Luxford, Griselda Yorke, Beth Byrne and Eleanor Lang) have maintained. Now that the company produces work in several countries, the role of the administrative office and tour personnel in realizing large-scale international tours on several different models is ever more important. The Russian model in particular, overseen by Russian producer Anya Kolesnikova, keeps productions in repertory for years, with perhaps one or two revivals a year, meaning that productions such as *Boris Godunov* and *Twelfth Night* have a particularly complex performance history.

Perhaps most importantly, though, Cheek by Jowl is the acting ensemble, central to a company ethos that is built around the craft of the actor, as expounded in *The Actor and the Target*. The particular requirements of Cheek by Jowl's work – the long international tours and the fully integrated ensemble practice that often has most company members on stage for the majority of the play's running time – mean that the company's casting practices prioritize establishing an ensemble who can work well together over individual stars (Byrne 2016). Infamously, Cheek by Jowl never holds open auditions, relying instead on trusted casting directors such as Siobhan Bracke and on established relationships. Orlando James recalls his audition thus:

If you're a new actor for them, they won't focus on the play. They'll just want to see how you perform, and how you react to direction, and how open you are to play. So you're just asked to learn a speech that relates to the subject matter of the play, or just the period, and you'll come and do that. Then, if you get a recall, then they'll start going into the thing, and at that point, you start to do it fully. You act opposite an actor; you prepare a scene or speech, and you have a partner to play it with and to work on it with, and Declan will be there and work with both of you as well. I was very surprised when I first started helping them with auditions that I was getting as much direction and notes as the person auditioning! Because that's just how he works – he creates that environment there. (James 2016)

In the UK, the company has often hired actors straight out of drama school, and the company is regularly spoken of as a 'training ground for British theatre' (Moreton 2016) or 'a nursery to young talent' (Rutter 2005: 346). The number of now-famous names who took major roles with Cheek by Jowl in one of their first jobs – Gwendoline Christie, Michelle Fairley, Amanda Harris, Tom Hiddleston, Anastasia Hille, Tom Hollander, Marianne Jean-Baptiste, Paterson Joseph, Adrian Lester, Matthew Macfadyen, Stephen Mangan, David Morrissey, Saskia Reeves, Michael Sheen, Olivia Williams – is indicative of the company's eye for promising talent and/or of the value of Cheek by Jowl in consolidating the young actor's craft, and this reputation led to the experiment of the RSC Academy in 2002, with Nonso Anozie playing a lauded Lear at the age of twenty-four. But the directors like to work repeatedly with valued collaborators. In the 1980s, the names of Keith Bartlett, Duncan Duff, Timothy Walker and Anne White appeared regularly; more recently, recurring collaborators in the English productions have included David Collings, Orlando James and Peter Moreton. This desire is met most successfully in the Russian and French work, where working practices and permanent ensembles have allowed Donnellan and Ormerod to work repeatedly with actors such as Alexander Feklistov and Andrei Kuzichev (Russia) and Camille Cayol, Christophe Grégoire, Xavier Boiffier and Cécile Leterme (France) for over a decade.

Personal relationships sit at the heart of Cheek by Jowl. As Donnellan writes:

> The idea of a family is important to me. A piece of theatre has to be moving in some way, and for that I need an emotional docking, not just with Nick but with all the people involved, where they turn up on time not because they're professionals, but because they've made an emotional commitment to the rest of the cast. (Curtis 1994)

Ormerod and Donnellan's own personal and professional relationship has remained central to the company's identity since the two founded it in 1981 as a way of establishing their creative partnership. Whether in the regular mentions of the pair's home, anecdotes about their car crashing on the way to their first Edinburgh production or in the constant inclusion of both men in interviews that would normally focus on a single director, Cheek by Jowl maintains the consistent message that the company is founded on a conversation, an exchange, an interaction.[9] In *A Midsummer Night's Dream*, the quotation that forms the company's name is preceded by Demetrius's statement (threat or promise) that 'I'll go with thee' (3.2.338); in Donnellan and Ormerod's unusual practice of following their touring productions to almost every venue over tours that can last years, they literally do.

This book

This book is not a comprehensive history of every Shakespeare production Cheek by Jowl has created, nor a study of Donnellan's acclaimed approach to acting – for which there is no better guide than *The Actor and the Target* itself, of which actor Xavier Boiffier says, 'really, it's him. It's not like intellectual theory, it's really about experience' (2016). Rather, what follows is a study of the symbiotic relationship between Cheek by Jowl and Shakespeare: what the company's productions of early modern drama illustrate of the company's practice, and what in turn Cheek by Jowl's work reveals about the plays of Shakespeare and his contemporaries. Most of the best writing hitherto on the company, such as that by Paul Prescott (2008), uses only brief descriptions of moments from several productions to trace broader techniques or ideas. By contrast, this book uses detailed case studies – two productions per chapter – to pursue the implications of Cheek by Jowl's practice for particular works in depth. My choices of focus are both pragmatic and arbitrary: this is not a 'best of' Cheek by Jowl, and I apologize to those whose favourite productions are not adequately represented. I prioritize productions from the 1990s onwards, as the first decade of the company's history is so eloquently covered by Simon Reade's *Cheek by Jowl: Ten Years of Celebration* (1991). I have myself seen all of Cheek by Jowl's productions since *Othello* (2004) live in the theatre, many several times, and have supplemented my own memories with recordings, promptbooks, tour reports and the correspondence of the company's archives, as well as new interviews with the company's alumni.[10]

Another danger that occurs when writing about Cheek by Jowl is the risk of canonizing individual performances. Among the many distinctive aspects of Cheek by Jowl's practices is that the production is never finished. While the assistant director, assistant stage manager and tour manager keep the show on the road, Donnellan and Ormerod drop in regularly to as many venues as they can, and all of the actors I have spoken to remark on the constant notes and re-rehearsal sessions, sometimes occurring as late as the third-to-last show before the end of a two-year tour. As Peter Moreton puts it, 'to my knowledge, there's no other company that has notes every night before a show' (2016). Adrian Lester goes further:

> The productions he directs are alive. He avoids 'fixing' his work. It keeps changing the more it is performed. Declan will come to see the production and the next day

during notes he will say 'Well, it looks like your belief is embedded in knowing what you're doing, so ... in that scene, why don't you come in from over there?' And that simple unrehearsed change reignites you and everyone on stage with you. It will be an unrehearsed physical moment surrounded by an emotional understanding that will play itself out fresh in front of the next night's audience. It really blows the cobwebs off. At other moments in notes sessions Declan will happily say 'I've never got that bit quite right, and I realised yesterday watching you after your seventieth performance that I know what I've done wrong', and then he'll completely redirect the scene for the better. He never stops working. (2016)

Donnellan and Ormerod's visibility and participation is a unique part of the Cheek by Jowl brand, and speaks to the company's unusual investment in the touring show as a constantly evolving work of art. The emphasis is on process and the lived moment, rather than on fixing a finished product; even the company's live recording of *Measure for Measure* was re-edited before being integrated into an education package (Kirwan 2018). The Cheek by Jowl production is more than usually inconstant and changing, fresh and flexible. The reader's own memories of seeing the productions I discuss will, I hope, both align with and vary interestingly from my own reports.

My first chapter spans the broadest range of Cheek by Jowl's history, with a particular eye on the developmental process of a production. I begin with the company's most recent English-language production, *The Winter's Tale* (2016–17). The company graciously allowed me to join them in the rehearsal room for a week, and my account of the production here introduces some of the preliminary work and experimentation that goes into creating a Cheek by Jowl production, including rehearsal methods, abandoned choices and underpinning ideas. That production's partial setting in Roscommon, where Donnellan grew up, serves as pretext to consider Cheek by

Jowl's process from a different angle, through analysis of the playtext of Donnellan's only self-penned original play for the company, *Lady Betty* (1989).[11] Separated by over a quarter of a century, the two productions' respective engagements with the rural Ireland of Donnellan's own youth are also revealing of the company's personal and emotional engagement with Shakespeare.

The remaining chapters take pairs of productions as the starting points for discussions of aspects of Cheek by Jowl's work. Chapter 2 concentrates on two of Cheek by Jowl's most celebrated productions of Jacobean tragedies: *The Duchess of Malfi* (1995–6) and *Macbeth* (2009–11). My account here takes its cue from the arresting opening images of both productions – an ensemble standing stock still on a dark stage, individuals surrounded by empty space. In this chapter, I theorize the company's distinctive use of space to both allow flexibility for and focus attention on the body of the actor, and I consider the interpretive choices that foreground the individual actor and their interactions. The recurrence of Anastasia Hille as the Duchess and Lady Macbeth allows for direct comparison of Cheek by Jowl's work with one actor fourteen years apart. In both productions, the isolation of the humans at the plays' centres allows the company to plumb the depths of human experience, to sometimes controversial effect, and this chapter argues that the interaction of space and bodies, with attention to the role of movement, is key to that effect.

In Chapter 3, I turn to two productions so successful that they have sometimes skewed representations of Cheek by Jowl as being an 'all-male company' (Power 2016: 68). *As You Like It* (1991–5), the company's tenth-anniversary production, remains Cheek by Jowl's best-known work, and arguably the most influential in inspiring a new generation of all-male Shakespeare in the work of Propeller and other companies. *Twelfth Night* (2003–) is Cheek by Jowl's most enduring production, with at least two performances in every calendar year until 2014 and a recast version returning to the repertory in 2016.[12] The two productions – one in English, the other in

Russian – share a substantial amount of DNA. As with *The Duchess of Malfi* and *Macbeth*, both introduced the entire ensemble at the top of the production, but here the actors appeared as blank shapes before being dressed in the costumes appropriate to their character and gender. In this chapter, I address the company's ground-breaking work with a single-gender cast in developing approaches to the performance of gender, and I consider the ways in which comedy leans on the interplay of the ensemble.

Chapter 4 concentrates on two productions from the company's loose 'cycle' of 'late romances' (Cheek by Jowl 2016). *Cymbeline* (2007) and *The Tempest* (2011–) serve as case studies for what I argue are the filmic qualities of Cheek by Jowl's approaches to text. Two hallmarks of Donnellan and Ormerod's style lend themselves to the language of film analysis: the visual interruption of a continuous scene by the appearance of other characters, normally those being discussed (the *cutaway*); and the overlapping of scenes, often introducing the first line of the following scene before the last line of the preceding scene (the *dissolve*). In this chapter, I use the promptbook of *Cymbeline* and archival recordings of *The Tempest* to introduce these elements of Cheek by Jowl's style, and I consider how the use of 'frozen' and 'projected' subjects creates visual emotional reference points within the ensemble production. The use of filmic language may seem surprising given Donnellan and Ormerod's unusual commitment to the stage, but I argue that their attention to intimacy and to the craft of the actor has allowed Cheek by Jowl to pioneer techniques that appropriate the perceived advantages of film in a medium that is wholly theatrical.[13]

In Chapter 5, I move on to the interplay of design and bodies in two recent productions of non-Shakespeare plays. *'Tis Pity She's a Whore* (2011–14) and *Ubu Roi* (2013–15) were both highly conceptual pieces that used more detailed and elaborate sets than is customary for the company: *'Tis Pity* brought all of the play's action into the confines of Annabella's poster-festooned bedroom, while *Ubu Roi* stuck to a bourgeois living/

dining room, captured in forensic detail by the live camera feed operated by a character throughout. These closed spaces enabled metanarratives of wish-fulfilment, juxtaposing the Cheek by Jowl style with environments that commented on, as well as complemented, the primary action. In this chapter, I examine the combination of comedy and violence that erupted in these two controversial plays, and I argue for the role of design in creating an attitude of serious irreverence. That these two plays both themselves respond to Shakespeare plays (*Romeo and Juliet* and *Macbeth*, respectively) in violent and visually striking ways allows these case studies to epitomize Cheek by Jowl's sometimes iconoclastic approach to classic texts.

For the sixth and final chapter, I draw together all of the elements hitherto discussed to offer thick readings of two final productions: **Much Ado about Nothing** (1998) and **Measure for Measure** (2013–). Here, my interest is in how the productions expound ideas of isolation and empathy, the latter word increasingly frequent in Donnellan's interviews. While the company may be most easily characterized by its stylistic and formal idiosyncrasies, this chapter prioritizes the depth of insight that emerges on all levels of a Cheek by Jowl production when a company is invested in attempting to understand and empathize with behaviours, typifying a company that finds something fresh in every moment.

Alongside these case studies, I gesture to other productions in Cheek by Jowl's history, as well as selected works by Ormerod and Donnellan that fall outwith the Cheek by Jowl purview, and the Appendix gives a full list of the company's productions for reference. The snapshots of the company's work contained within these chapters cannot hope to be exhaustive, but they do, I hope, go some way towards making the case for Cheek by Jowl being one of the most significant and consistent interpreters of Shakespeare working today.

1

Shakespeare of Roscommon: tracing a Cheek by Jowl production

The Winter's Tale (2016–17) and *Lady Betty* (1989)

The gap of time

14 January 2016. As the audience shuffled into Les Geméaux in Sceaux, Paris, they were met by an anoraked, hooded figure sitting on a low white box, facing upstage away from the audience. This figure (Grace Andrews) was revealed later to be Time, pulling off her hood to reveal flowing blonde hair; at the start of the play she was merely an anonymous figure who was, or had been, waiting. The premiere of this production came some eighteen years after Donnellan and Ormerod's previous production of *The Winter's Tale* opened at the Maly Theatre in St Petersburg; the time-jump is poetically close to the play's own 'gap of time' (5.3.154). I begin with *The Winter's Tale* as the company's most recent English-language production and

as one whose strong creative, interpretive and personal ties to the company's past makes it a fitting place to enter Cheek by Jowl's process.

The company's past was evoked both onstage and off. The 2016 production's opening echoed that of their Russian production, in which a shawled babushka figure (Tatyana Rasskazova) appeared onstage first before sweeping her way through the celebrating nobility.[1] In another link with the company's past, it reunited several of the company's longest-serving collaborators, with Paddy Cunneen returning as musical director for the first time since *Homebody/Kabul* (2001–2), along with Judith Greenwood (lighting designer) and Jane Gibson (associate and movement director).[2] Finally, this was the first Cheek by Jowl production set (partly) in Ireland since Donnellan's self-penned play *Lady Betty* (1989), set in the Roscommon of Donnellan's own childhood. As *Lady Betty* had cast former Irish dancing champions (Reade 1991: 36), so too did *The Winter's Tale* feature several Irish actors, lending local specificity to the production's depiction of Bohemia.

But while the production looked back, *The Winter's Tale* was also indicative of the company's ongoing innovation. This was one of the first Cheek by Jowl productions to have a specific set constructed prior to the start of rehearsals – a large white box with opening panels on all sides – building on the company's recent explorations of detailed visual design in *'Tis Pity She's a Whore* and *Ubu Roi* (see Chapter 5). It was the first English-language production to include the option of a live-streamed performance in the company's contracts (Lang 2017). And it also trialled a new touring model for the UK company based on experiences with the Russian and French companies: the run began with a three-month tour of Europe before going on hiatus for several months, allowing the cast to pursue other projects, after which the company reformed to complete the tour.[3] The production's first dates in the UK took place well over a year after the first performance.

I sat in on a week of rehearsals, meaning that this chapter will focus primarily on the development of a Cheek by Jowl production before opening.[4] In tracing some of the production's ideas from initial inception to public performance, I place a greater emphasis than in other chapters on rejected decisions and rehearsal room processes, insights rarely available to me for other productions. I then turn to another pre-performance record: the script for *Lady Betty*, the story of the notorious hangwoman of Roscommon and the only self-penned play and narrative designed explicitly for Cheek by Jowl. In pairing *The Winter's Tale* with *Lady Betty*, I am wary of creating misleading or overly neat narratives. However, the explicit references to Roscommon in *The Winter's Tale* rehearsal room and the reuse of incidental music to inform the tone of the scenes do suggest at least an external tonal connection. By linking these two productions, this chapter will consider some of Cheek by Jowl's core processes as the work begins to emerge.

Rehearsing *The Winter's Tale*

Donnellan does not teach people how to act. As Owen Horsley says, 'the coach doesn't doubt that his footballers can play football – that's something that's a given. But there are rules within the pitch that the coach's job is to teach them … It's about how to react to the play, how to respond to the world that we're creating' (2016). The rehearsal period is a genuine process of discovery for all concerned, and is built from the start around the bodies of the actors.

Cheek by Jowl rehearsals never start with a table read. Donnellan begins the rehearsal process with movement: *As You Like It* (1991) began with a tango, while *Cymbeline* (2007) started with step dancing (Sierz 2010: 155). Such work serves multiple functions. The tango, for instance, is 'a very political dance about who is in control, which is a key question in the play' (Donnellan 1999: 20), but the work also 'strengthened backs, brought the company together, focused us, and was not wasted' (Sierz 2010: 155).

Horsley notes that 'when you teach a dance to a bunch of actors, they're all at the same level – unless someone's an expert Flamenco dancer [the dance used for *The Changeling* (2006)]. Whereas if you sit around a table with Shakespeare, you instantly make a hierarchical shift between the abilities of people in the room' (2016). A process such as this furthers the development of the ensemble ethos, prioritizing collaborative interaction. The morning warm-ups at the start of each rehearsal are led by a different actor each day, organizing games that get the actors' bodies moving before the directors arrive, and at the rehearsals I observed (relatively late in the process) the actors then went on to movement work with Jane Gibson before Donnellan took over to address specific scenes.

Cheek by Jowl's work is rooted in text. The company does not devise work in the sense that might characterize contemporaries such as Complicité, and *The Actor and the Target* devotes a long closing section to interpreting verse (Donnellan 2005: 245–72). A well-thumbed Arden 2 edition of *The Winter's Tale* sat on the production table throughout rehearsal, and the actors understood every word; Donnellan requires that actors are off-book by the time rehearsals begin, a demand he recognizes as unusual (Donnellan 1999: 19). But the text is only a strand of the rehearsal room experience, and Peter Moreton suggests that 'they don't let you think about it for a long period at the beginning of rehearsal. It's kind of barred from the room ... It's the approach of the text being abstract in terms of being vowels and syllables instead of words and poetry – it takes it to its core level of the human, emotional element of it' (2016). The process privileges feeling over form, and the text itself is negotiable. If lines distract from the spirit of the play, they are removed; if sense can be clarified by the substitution of a word (provided it preserves the metre), that decision will be made without fear.[5] What the company seeks isn't an ever-more-rarefied textual exegesis but an experience of aliveness, of humans relating to one another in space, which the text must serve.

During the rehearsals I observed, Donnellan sat on a chair with nothing separating him from the actors. Ormerod was to his immediate right, Gibson to his left and the assistant director (Marcus Roche) an arm's reach away on the other side of Gibson. Gibson is not present for the whole run of rehearsals, describing herself to me as 'on call' throughout the run (Gibson 2016); Donnellan describes her as 'one of the great unsung heroes/heroines of British theatre … I really depend on Jane in Britain. She helps the actors' bodies to move and to experience things in their bodies' (Donnellan 2009: 86). Ormerod and Donnellan work with trusted collaborators, and the physical positioning of the team rendered them a striking single unit. The close clustering of the creative team's bodies and their proximity to the performance space allowed Donnellan to launch Gibson or himself physically into the scene whenever they needed to illustrate a point physically. But for the most part, Donnellan was a watcher and commentator with undivided focus on the actors; Adrian Lester reports Donnellan telling him in rehearsal, 'I only open my mouth if I don't believe it, and as I take a breath in to speak I have to understand why I don't believe it, and that's my only job' (Lester 2016). The actors (at least by this stage of rehearsal) were trusted to run the scene, and Donnellan intervened when necessary. Natalie Radmall-Quirke remembers Donnellan telling her early in the process, 'I'm not an acting teacher, I'm a coach' (2016). In his own writings, Donnellan repeatedly characterizes his role as responsive: 'Normally the acting starts off rather dull; then, after a while, it gets more interesting, and I spend my time waiting and watching for the actors' inventiveness' (Sierz 2010: 154). The impression to the external observer is of Donnellan as an acute observer of human interaction, who shapes the production by offering feedback on what is and is not working.

Donnellan's book *The Actor and the Target* offers the fullest published account of his approach to acting and is best read in full rather than summary. The purpose of the book is not to explain how he directs a production or interprets Shakespeare, but to address one of the fundamental problems of the actor's experience – when fear blocks the ability to act. His much-discussed 'target' is not a focus or an objective (Donnellan 2005: 27), but a practical method of rearticulating where the energy of the scene lies, which is always external to the actor 'so that we can then bounce off it, react to it and live off it' (24). Donnellan understands his role as being to remove the blocks that prevent actors responding organically to the predicament of the space (his currently preferred terms), rather than to tell them what to do. For Donnellan, this is as fundamental as breathing:

> All we can be 'taught' about acting are double negatives. For example, we can be taught how *not* to block our natural instinct to act, just as we can be taught how *not* to block our natural instinct to breathe … this is not a book about how to act; this is a book that may help when you feel blocked in your acting. (2005: 2–3)

This is why there is relatively little direct instruction in the rehearsal room. The positions of actors relative to one another change substantially from run to run, according to where the scene takes the actors, and Declan asks for several runs in order to allow the actors to try out different ideas. 'Declan's concept,' suggests Orlando James, 'is freedom for the actors' (2016). He notes when things are not working and when something interesting has happened, but when something interesting happens, the actors are not then required to replicate that precise sequence. This results in a fast-paced rehearsal, with many different versions of a scene generated within a short space of time and a great many ideas rejected. The assistant director and deputy stage manager annotate their copies constantly, but the principle here is not that the actors should remember which of these worked most effectively and then reproduce it; the point is that the most interesting, the most *live* performances emerge from the actors being free. This does not mean that there are not rules specific to particular productions; for example, Cécile Leterme recalls that when working on

Andromaque, 'the stage was something that had to be balanced … The movements were free as long as the stage was balanced always' (2016). But the shared experience is of the actors generating performance that Donnellan watches and shapes.

Two of his most important practical tools are the anecdote and the *étude*. The *étude* is an approach that recurs in conversation with actors who have worked in English, French or Russian with Cheek by Jowl. Deriving from Stanislavski's techniques of active analysis and 'acting with the body' (Innes and Shevtsova 2013: 74), *études* are improvisations that the actors prepare away from Donnellan and Ormerod.

> We will discuss a scene – say the convent – and ask the actors to present a scene from life in the convent. These normally occur 'in the woods' when we might be staying in some interesting wreck of a house. The actors normally find some site-specific corner to show some aspect of the play. Preferably there are no words and little unexpected incident. The best outcome is that the actors surprise us. (Donnellan 2018)

Sometimes *études* help establish backstories and relationships. Joy Richardson (Paulina) describes a two-hour improvisation with Radmall-Quirke (Hermione) imagining the years of Hermione's seclusion:

> It starts with me trying to get her to move, get her to want to live, get her out of this state of being comatose out of shock. One thing that came to mind in the moment was a little bird that hopped into my place. And I draw her attention to it, and she keeps this bird as a pet, and she has to feed the bird … it gives her a purpose to nurture, to come back. And little treats and laughter come back – and laughter's part of the cure for her. (Richardson 2016)

Work such as this regularly takes place away from the rehearsal room, as part of the actors' 'homework', developing character relationships that then feed into the main explorations. At other times, though, *études* were worked through in the rehearsal room as a way of boiling down the scene to its core essence, before being integrated as implicit emotional reference points into the main scene. Two examples I observed will illustrate.

Key to the exploration of Bohemia was the discovery made concerning this passage, spoken by the Old Shepherd.

> Fie, daughter! when my old wife lived, upon
> This day she was both pantler, butler, cook,
> Both dame and servant; welcomed all, served all;
> Would sing her song and dance her turn; now here,
> At upper end o' the table, now i' the middle;
> On his shoulder, and his; her face o' fire
> With labour and the thing she took to quench it,
> She would to each one sip. You are retired,
> As if you were a feasted one and not
> The hostess of the meeting.
>
> (4.4.55–64)

The Shepherd's speech berates his (adopted) daughter for not managing to fully live up to the detailed picture he paints of his dead wife's idealized performance of hospitality. The company imagined that 'when my old wife lived' might refer to the previous year's feast, suggesting that the speech was inspired by the rawness of the memory for all of the bereaved family.

For the *étude*, Donnellan asked Joy Richardson to play the Shepherd's wife, joining Peter Moreton (Shepherd), Eleanor McLoughlin (Perdita) and Sam McArdle (Clown) to go through the motions of preparing for the previous year's festival. Using the same spatial restrictions already established for the scene, the mother ran the preparations and, as the *étude* progressed, Donnellan invited the actors to effectively ignore one another, implying the quiet familiarity of a close family that meant preparations ran like clockwork, with the family barely needing to look at or speak to one another. The actors fell into easy rhythms of passing objects from one to another, putting small tasks aside to assist with larger items and becoming easy with one another's company. Then, Richardson was removed from the scene. Suddenly, the remaining family members had to go through the process for the first time without the mother, turning the mother into a present absence that led to awkwardness, discomfort and heightened emotions as the characters attempted to reorganize their accustomed tasks.

When the company returned to the text, the Shepherd's outburst against Perdita had become one of the most important speeches of the Bohemia scenes, putting the undercurrent of sadness into words. As soon as the Shepherd mentioned 'my old wife', both son and daughter ran quickly to their father, hushing and comforting him out of care and embarrassment; it was clear that this was not the first time the Shepherd had opened up about his grief, but perhaps the first time he had done so in front of non-family members. Moreton remembers that 'suddenly "lived" has a different meaning … we'd normally say "my wife before she died". Joy is one of the most alive people on the planet, and it carries in. I don't think I'd have landed on that observation of the line without the *étude*' (2016). The absence of the wife and mother lent a melancholy air to Bohemia and foregrounded the loss of family that pervades *The Winter's Tale*, providing an unusually strong thematic connection between this scene and the rest of the play.

My second example is a much simpler sequence based on 4.2, in which Abubakar Salim's Camillo announced to Edward Sayer's Polixenes his intention to return to Sicilia. The dynamic of this scene was reworked several times in the days of rehearsal that I witnessed, with a suitcase becoming a particular object of contention as Camillo placed his suitcase on the ground, Polixenes took it and the two negotiated for its possession. An *étude* sought to clarify an important part of Donnellan's practice – the stakes. As Donnellan puts it in *The Actor and the Target*:

The stakes are so important they have their own double rule. The unbreakable double rule is as follows: 1. At every living moment there is something to be lost and something to be won. 2. The thing to be won is precisely the same size as the thing to be lost. (Donnellan 2005: 51)

The stark example is for Juliet: '*that I will run away with Romeo and that I will not run away with Romeo*' (Donnellan 2005: 51), the potential gain and loss of exactly equal significance. Xavier Boiffier describes it as one of Declan's 'fundamental demands ... that the stakes are super high' (2016). Here, Camillo is trying to return to Sicilia *and* trying to not be detained in Bohemia; Polixenes is fighting to keep Camillo in Bohemia *and* fighting not to be left alone in Bohemia. What is to be won and lost for each man is of equal importance, leading to a push/pull dynamic. The *étude* was 'a trick to get into the scene' (Donnellan and Ormerod 2016) that reduced their interactions to a single phrase each: Polixenes saying, 'Don't go,' followed by Camillo saying, 'I must go.' Paddy Cunneen, in the rehearsal room at the time, cued up Rachmaninoff's 'Piano Concerto No. 2', with the music, famous from *Brief Encounter*, standing for the deep swell of emotion residing behind the stiff upper lips of these two reserved characters. As the two men circled one another repeating 'Don't go'/'I must go,' the tug of power between them became palpable and continued to inform the dynamic once the actors returned to the text.

The primary purpose of the *étude* is to clarify the emotional stakes of a scene, to release what is there to be won and lost. One of the most distinctive features of Cheek by Jowl's practice is that each scene is subjected to the same care and scrutiny to find out what the stakes are, and therefore even a simple sequence such as Camillo offering to leave becomes fraught with urgency, pathos and desperation. This does not lead to simplistic productions; quite the contrary. But with the foundational stakes established, the actors are free to uncover new meaning in the text.

Donnellan's anecdotes are part of the process of discovery, and he admits that the anecdote is an increasingly important part of his mode of communication in rehearsal.

It's a means by which I talk elliptically. I tell a story, and the story is enigmatic, so it's something that will spark off something in [the actors'] imaginations. I remember as a tiny child a visit from the story tellers … There were two old men who knocked at nights at my grandmother's tiny farmhouse, deep in the pre-electrified Irish countryside – and for some whiskey they would slowly tell amazing stories. No one would ever interrupt. And they stilled me and my boisterous uncles as we looked deeper into the fire … Or perhaps I dreamed it … I manage now without the whiskey but find storytelling a comfortable and effective way to direct – I'll tell stories, tangentially connected to [the scene], and then I'll ask the actors to do an *étude* on the basis of the play. But if they have been taken by the story they will think of the situation in another way. A way that will surprise us all. (Donnellan and Ormerod 2016)

Actors speak of the approach warmly; as Richardson notes, 'They give you such a clear example and clarity' (2016), and James suggests that the stories unlock the actor: 'Through him sharing his stories about [injustice], I was able to step back from my own. He has a way of opening things up for different people' (2016). For Owen Horsley, this is one of the most revolutionary parts of Donnellan's practice.

He's just interested in people's experience, and he always imagines what it would be like to be in that … And sometimes he has a very emotional response to it … He'll never come up with an answer about what he feels about [for instance] abandonment, but he feels it. And if the play is somehow connected to that, then that will very clearly and very unfiltered go into the play and the production itself. Which I think is incredibly brave … and very, very rare. (2016)

Donnellan makes explicit to the company early in the rehearsal process that he will tell a lot of stories, but that this is not an invitation or instruction for the company to share their own stories in response. Donnellan is not an auteur in terms of imposing a rigid style on a production, but the productions are informed by his outlook on the world and by the experiences he shares with his company. These range from moral stories and historical explanations of concepts to personal experiences and his own philosophy. The short scene between Cleomenes and Dion returning from the Oracle (3.1), for instance, occasioned an explanation of pilgrimage as an internal and external journey, one endured, which changes the destination depending on how one reaches it; the explanation fed into a conception of the scene as something that had exhausted them, emotionally and physically. In discussing the Bohemia scenes, Donnellan offered a series of personal anecdotes about social awkwardness, from the deep disquiet of poorly organized funerals to watching an argument on the Tube between strangers that threatened to spiral out of control. Then later, as the company approached the trial scenes, he talked extensively about his own conception of grace, in the sense of whether humans can do good by themselves; as he pointed out, we cannot insist upon grace. This last, as he explained, 'isn't something to play, it's something to understand'. Donnellan doesn't tell his actors how to behave, but he asks them to share his understanding of what is at stake in any given moment. What emerges from that will inform the production.

Finding the stakes in *The Winter's Tale*

The actor cannot play the stakes, in the sense that the stakes are one thing that can be created. Instead the actor needs to see the big two, both what may be lost and also what may be won. So remember that whenever the expression 'the stakes' is used, it never describes a state. The stakes are always two directions in conflict. There is always something to be lost and always something to be won. (Donnellan 2005: 54)

As discussed in the previous section, an important aspect of Cheek by Jowl rehearsal is finding the stakes of the scene – or rather, freeing up actors in order that they can play the stakes as they emerge and shift throughout the course of the play. A key point in the above quotation is that the stakes are not 'a state' that can be played, but the things that the character stands to win and lose. The character's stakes are not the same as the actor's, and if the actor can see what is at stake for the character, they can respond freely. In this section, I use my own observations from *The Winter's Tale* rehearsals to illustrate this theory in practice.

For the trial scene (2.2), Donnellan and Ormerod returned to some of the thinking that informed their 1997 production. That production set up a simple podium and a microphone, with Hermione (Natalya Akimova) exposed in the centre to give her testimony, while Leontes (Petr Semak) sat downstage left, facing away from his wife. The Russian version was austere, with all the bodies separated throughout the trial, and Leontes only shifting position when he marched across to tear up the oracle; in that production, Leontes' performed rigidity and isolation occasioned the tragedy. For the 2016 production, Donnellan and Ormerod used a similar structure (only now with a podium and a video screen to allow even greater scrutiny of Hermione's ordeal) but found new routes through the scene to reconnect the emotional arcs of all the participants.

In preparing the trial scene, Donnellan told Natalie Radmall-Quirke (Hermione) that she must be totally unaware of the structure of the scene or its possible outcome. Hermione cannot know how long she will be allowed to speak for; the actor must be surprised by her own speeches and not know what is coming next.[6] The stakes for the whole ensemble in this scene could not be higher – Leontes' irrational behaviour means that the assembled company is driven by the terror of no longer knowing what might happen. Donnellan gave a rare technical note at this point, asking Radmall-Quirke not to release her breath at the end of her speeches; while the *actor* may have completed a gruelling set piece, the stakes are still rising for the *character*. My rehearsal notes below trace three takes on one section – the reactions to the prophecy (104–38).

> TAKE ONE: Beginning from Hermione's line, 'Now, my liege, / Tell me what blessings I have here alive' (104–5), the company played through Hermione's call for the oracle and its reading. The blocking was roughly symmetrical: Leontes stood alone at stage right; Hermione surrounded by her women at stage left; the First Lord (Chris Gordon) central at a podium. As the First Lord read the oracle, the bodies on both sides of the stage collapsed simultaneously. Gibson intervened to arrange Hermione's women into a kneeling position, facing Hermione; the resulting image was of two fragile people, Leontes alone and Hermione surrounded by support. After the oracle was completed, Donnellan asked Radmall-Quirke to take control of the scene by coming to re-read for herself the last, confusing sentence of the oracle: 'the king shall live without an heir, if that which is lost be not found' (132–3). He wanted to explore the relative strangeness of the final enigmatic statement following the clear verdicts of innocence and guilt; this fairy-tale riddle here does not align with what comes before. Having Hermione read this line didn't lead to anything immediately, but Donnellan then asked what might be at stake if this last pronouncement was delayed – mundanely, perhaps it is over the page, so that the First Lord does not initially see it.

> TAKE TWO: Before beginning the scene, Gibson and Donnellan adjusted the way that Hermione's women supported her in her collapse – now they held her hands rather than her arms, in a more empathetic gesture. As the First Lord read the prophecy, Hermione gave an enormous, vindicated shout of laughter, her hands tightening around those of her attendants, as her innocence was proclaimed. The laugh then halted on the pronouncement that Leontes was a 'jealous tyrant', introducing a moment of audible

uncertainty. The First Lord stopped reading the oracle after 'his innocent babe truly begotten' (132). In the silence that followed, Hermione slowly stood, crossed the stage to Leontes and paused. Then she gently touched her husband, who remained prostrate on the floor. After this, the prophecy continued. Donnellan noted that this new version opened up the possibility of grace, putting the spotlight on Hermione as she offered forgiveness magnanimously. James responded by pleading for and even accepting forgiveness, and the room was allowed a moment of hope and peace as husband and wife embraced. But then the final line of the prophecy, now an ambivalent 'PS', cut across this moment. In the first experiment with this idea, Leontes' 'Hast thou read truth?' (135) was a sincere and confused question. Leontes had accepted his error and publicly humbled himself, but the assertion that he had no heir made no sense: he has Mamillius. This apparent error in the prophecy vindicated his suspicions, allowing him to question the oracle and dismiss the whole: 'There is no truth at all i'the oracle' was pronounced with relief; he angrily snatched and tore the paper up. Donnellan realized they had made a major discovery, and the company agreed to work it through.

TAKE THREE: For the third pass at this sequence, Donnellan gave the ensemble two suggestions. Firstly, he asked them to respond individually to each part of the oracle. This is typical of Cheek by Jowl's approach to text – rather than treat it as one homogeneous delivered report, Declan looked for the individual reactions to each part of the prophecy. Secondly, he asked the whole ensemble to lay hands on Leontes after the oracle's apparent conclusion. During this run, Gordon's reading of the prophecy came to life. The women cried out in joy on 'Hermione is chaste'; Leontes sank further on 'Polixenes blameless'; there was even laughter trivializing the almost irrelevant point 'Camillo a true subject,' the half-forgotten collateral damage of Leontes' jealousy. Leontes was left prostrate in tears. Slowly, the company formed the image Declan requested – Hermione walked over and laid her hand on him, then Paulina, then the rest of the company. Amid this quietness, Leontes called out a muffled 'Apollo be praised.' The image of the ensemble crouched and close to one another mirrored one that was ultimately used at the end of the production, and in the rehearsal room it was allowed to form slowly. Only after an extended pause did Gordon then complete the prophecy, causing everyone to raise their heads in confusion, their emotion interrupted. Leontes went across to the podium quietly to take the prophecy. At this point, the rest of the ensemble began standing, and Donnellan called out to remind them that nothing bad had happened yet. Leontes read the prophecy for himself, and only then tore the paper, at which the ensemble cried out in shock.

By the time the production reached its first public performances, the activity of the whole ensemble had been stripped back to concentrate on the primary connection: that between Hermione and Leontes. The introduction of the video screen, absent in rehearsals, was important here, as it meant that Hermione's speech was accompanied by an enlarged image of her face filling the stage, privileging her experience. She alone crossed to Leontes and the two held one another, Leontes sobbing in bursts of defeat, until the Lord read the final, belated line of the prophecy. But the process that the company underwent with this scene in the rehearsal room (of which my description here is, of course, only partial) freed up a series of possibilities and ideas that reinforced for everyone in the room the stakes. For Hermione in particular, the stakes visibly shifted – her need to defend herself against accusation, culminating in her reaction to the life-saving words of the oracle; her need to reach out to and fix her broken husband; her need to understand the enigmatic final words of the prophecy; her need to again rein in a situation that threatened to spiral out of hand; her final reaction to the news of Mamillius's death. For Leontes, the stakes shifted less – the need to be vindicated was paused by the first words of the oracle, leaving him a mess of paralysed reaction, until the final words of the oracle reasserted the very goal he had been pursuing. And the shifting stakes for each of these two were reflected in the courtiers around them. Cheek by Jowl actors do not stand waiting for a cue, but are required to be constantly responding to what is happening in the room and to what they need of others.

Body and view

Orlando James explains that, in the rehearsal room, the company had considered Leontes as perhaps suffering from a form of 'borderline personality disorder … it's swinging from black to white and back again with zero greyness' (2016). An exploration of psychiatric illness is not atypical of productions of *The Winter's Tale*;[7] however, this often leads to productions that invite the audience into Leontes' headspace, to share his perspective. The greatest pressure for such productions is how to visualize the (imagined) external trigger for Leontes' behaviour without going some way towards exculpating him. Productions regularly put Hermione and Polixenes into slow-motion as they touch one another, exaggerating their kissing or holding hands, or even acting out in full Leontes' projected fears. However far such moments are encoded as Leontes' point of view, they nevertheless force the audience to experience and momentarily share his view. Such moments create an ethical difficulty: how can a production simultaneously create a logical visualization of Leontes' thought process while not colluding in victim-blaming?

Cheek by Jowl's abstracted aesthetic allowed for a creatively rich solution that, as in the above sequences, clarified the stakes. During the opening scene, Leontes, Polixenes and Hermione shared a bench, imagining a domestic relationship while divorcing the bodies' interactions from any literal environment; a moment Arantxa Vela notes also stripped down the party of the 1997 production to the central conflict, 'the triangle that provokes the drama' (2016). As Leontes slipped into soliloquy

(1.2.108), Judith Greenwood's lighting shifted subtly to a green tint, while an eerie sound cue and James's upwardly tilted head indicated a different psychic space. Polixenes and Hermione sat perfectly still, facing forward, hands in laps. As Leontes began explaining what he 'saw', he created the thing he imagined by manipulating the others' bodies as if mannequins. This started relatively innocuously, even drawing laughter as he placed Hermione's hand on Polixenes' crotch while the two remained expressionless. Then, as Leontes' passion grew, he picked Hermione up and placed her on top of Polixenes, and set them thrusting into one another. Then he spun Hermione round so she straddled the bench, leaning forward, her pregnant belly on its surface, and moved Polixenes to embrace her from behind. Leontes thrust his own groin into Polixenes from behind, who in turn began mechanically thrusting into Hermione. The sequence literalized Nora Johnson's reading of the 'erotic compromise' of the two kings who have 'abandon[ed] physical immediacy for "mature dignity"' and who 'collaborate in the staging of Hermione as a necessary expression of their relationship' (1998: 199–200). But it also made clear that the behaviours Leontes describes were projections; any sense of a 'real' Hermione and Polixenes was entirely removed from this space. In portraying the scene in this way, the production removed any temptation to an 'objective' reading of the situation. The question of whether Hermione's behaviour was unimpeachable or not was simply irrelevant; this wasn't an issue of interpreting a woman's actions, but an issue of Leontes' own making. As James puts it, 'it's a much higher stakes choice to say "no, of course not." Because then that means that he has entirely brought that upon himself, which shoots through the play like an arrow to the end, with the retribution' (2016). Domestic violence, this production seemed to say, is entirely the responsibility of the perpetrator.

The manipulation of others within psychic space is an important recurring feature of Cheek by Jowl's work, which I will return to in future chapters. While it is now a trademark of contemporary productions of early modern drama, Cheek by

Jowl has always placed a strong emphasis on the visualization of characters when they are mentioned by others. Space is arranged not according to architectural logic, but instead is built around the direct connections between characters, and this foundational level of spatial organization requires bodies to be physically juxtaposed even when characters are not occupying the same diegetic environment. Cheek by Jowl has several strategies for enabling this, including the regular presence of the full ensemble on stage in any given production, the overlapping of scenes and the use of choric motifs to introduce actors before they take on character. The example under discussion here is a relatively straightforward instance, but the aesthetic beauty of the scene as the three bodies came into contact with one another, juxtaposed with the horror of what Leontes was creating, demonstrates the power of Cheek by Jowl's use of psychic space.

Revisiting Roscommon

The Bohemia scenes of *The Winter's Tale*, especially 4.4, frequently cause productions a headache as they struggle to work out what do with them. Too often the sheep-shearing festival becomes a loose framework for a series of disconnected entertainments, as in the near-simultaneous West End production by the Kenneth Branagh Company (2015), which rendered the scenes static and pageant-like, as shepherds waited silently for a series of dances.

In Cheek by Jowl's production, by contrast, anything not directly relevant to the emotional aspects of the scene was rejected. The party prioritized the emotional loss of the unseen mother as a local community gathered on a rainy afternoon to drink and celebrate together. Ryan Donaldson's Autolycus interrupted the elegiac party by bounding through the audience with a microphone and opened up an impromptu bazaar that sold a selection of headdresses and prank props, which the assorted revellers pounced on. Autolycus was the catalyst for a series of revelations that tore the party apart. First, Mopsa and Dorcas (Richardson and Radmall-Quirke literally letting their hair down) began a fight over one of the baubles, informed by their unspoken feud over the Clown. Autolycus offered to resolve the fight by parodying a Jeremy Kyle-style TV show, with live camera documenting the reactions of the Clown and women as Mopsa revealed her pregnancy. Despite the Clown pleading that his dad not be told, the Shepherd marched in, and Perdita was asked for her point of view. Hearing her unfilial judgement that the Clown should be made to choose, the Clown petulantly burst out with the revelation, 'You're not even my real sister!'

The Jeremy Kyle device was designed to both be comic and replace the entertainments of the sheep-shearing with something more pertinent to the characters' relationships. By having Perdita's true origins revealed to her *during* the scene, the production made clear the unspoken secret that lingered over those scenes. The Shepherd's grief over his wife laid open raw emotions that then translated into violent and aggressive revelations, and Perdita's own loss of her mother suddenly became the loss of her own family at exactly the same moment as she came together with Florizel (she immediately sought solace as the two started stripping off before being interrupted by Camillo). Throughout the sheep-shearing, the audience was invited to see the Clown and Perdita as real siblings who had grown up together – bickering, jostling and arguing. As they prepared for the party, they put each other in headlocks, hacked phlegm into one another's ears and pinched one another (Figure 1). This meant that, when this sibling bickering spilled over into genuine resentment during the party, the revelation carried serious emotional weight.

The sense of community, repression and emotional outburst was much discussed in the rehearsal room, particularly in relation to the stereotypes and lived experience of the Irish members of the cast. With the Shepherd and his family on display and the memories of lost loved ones still raw, the party

FIGURE 1 *Transition between 4.2 and 4.4. Camillo (Abubakar Salim), Old Shepherd (Peter Moreton), Perdita (Eleanor McLoughlin), Florizel (Chris Gordon), Sam McArdle (Clown) and Polixenes (Edward Sayer). Photograph by Johan Persson/ArenaPAL; www.arenapal.com.*

became a catalyst for outpourings of honesty. The setting was never meant to be a depiction of Ireland – Ormerod and Donnellan are adamant that 'it's not authentically Irish, it's authentically its own thing' (Donnellan and Ormerod 2016) – but having cast Donaldson, McArdle, McLoughlin and Radmall-Quirke, the Irish milieu presented itself. Radmall-Quirke (2016) notes the constructed aspects of this version of Ireland, her own accent wandering from Roscommon in the earlier rural scenes to something more Dublin-orientated for the Jeremy Kyle sequence, the location fantastical even as it evoked an imagined reality.

This was Cheek by Jowl's first production set in Ireland (even a fantastical one) since *Lady Betty* (1989), Donnellan's play on the legend of a Roscommon hangwoman, 'the local bogeyman' of his childhood (Donnellan and Ormerod 2016). Set in 1790, the impoverished 'Lady' Betty was arrested for killing her own son but, in exchange for her own life, took up the role of hangwoman when the regular hangman failed to turn up. She performed the role into the early nineteenth century. 'Always on the borders of madness, she drew each of her victims in charcoal before his execution' (Cheek by Jowl 1989a). The marketing material, which specifically targeted local Irish communities, put the Irish content at the forefront:

> An insight is also provided into the social history of 18th century rural Ireland, which was remarkable for its inequality, repression and poverty, but also for the strength of the people who lived through it. It is Ireland at the time of the Whiteboys, Wolfe Tone and the threat (or the promise) of invasion by Napoleon. Lady Betty herself is a memorable symbol of the Irish people's powers of resistance and survival. (Cheek by Jowl 1989b)

Lady Betty played to capacities averaging 43 per cent, low for Cheek by Jowl, but favourable in comparison to other new work (Cheek by Jowl 1991a: 2). The production played for only four months in late 1989, and only in the UK, placing it among Cheek by Jowl's least-seen works. Yet the experience of writing a play was important for Donnellan: 'Writing my own stuff was helpful for all the work I've later done, because then you realise the pragmatism of writing … It's very interesting to see the process of writing for a company and trying to get the story on stage with certain actors, which alters your perspective on the text' (Donnellan and Ormerod 1996: 89). Even in a play specifically set in Roscommon, *Lady Betty*'s enigmatic and semi-mythic text contextualizes the performative idea of Ireland that Donnellan and Ormerod returned to in *The Winter's Tale*.

Cheek by Jowl's typical approach of envisaging the ensemble together onstage is made explicit in *Lady Betty* as a 'Chorus' arrives together en masse, dressed similarly. The Chorus sing together, establishing what follows as a 'story':

Who will listen to our story?
Who will hear what we must tell?
Who will ride with us to glory?
Who will share our horse to hell? (Donnellan 1989: 3)

The play's opening puts the Chorus into tension with Betty, a structure reminiscent of that used for *Measure for Measure*, described in my introduction. They sing her story as a folk song and parable, a treatment that she both embraces and resists:

CHORUS SINGS
>   Lady Betty likes to draw
>   The face before it drops the jaw.
>   Pray to Jesus that she might
>   Not smile upon your face tonight

BETTY
>   And is that it all? Is that all me now? Broken words?
>   Flesh it for them. Pump it with blood the way I was young.
>   Dance my story in the dirt.   [*They dance*]
>   Harder, harder … …
>   [*The chorus dress two of their number as Lord John and Lady Sarah and Betty as an eighteenth century shepherdess*]

The emergence of individual characters from the ensemble is key to Cheek by Jowl's distinctive style. Donnellan has 'always naturally gravitated towards a chorus' (Donnellan and Ormerod 2016), and here the staging privileges the chorus of Irish keeners that produces Lady Betty from within itself; the play acknowledges Betty's crimes but points the finger at a society that creates her through neglect, fear and prejudice. The Chorus remains onstage throughout the play, producing new members of the Roscommon community as needed. As Betty sings her son, Oliver, to sleep the Chorus intervenes:

BETTY
Shall I sing you into a sleep as deep as peace itself?
MAN
Shut out her song
WOMAN
It will send you on a journey whose destination is further
than Roscommon,
MAN
Or London
WOMAN
Or Peace itself. (21)

The lightness of punctuation is telling of the speed and fluidity
that Donnellan anticipates. The play renders epic the humdrum
rural squat where Betty lives among the swine; she speaks
in poetry and elicits choric commentary. The community of
gossip-mongers that ostracizes her becomes a subjective,
omniscient chorus. In this semi-mundane, semi-mythological
space, psychic projections and the fantastical interweave with
the quotidian. The characters of Night, Cold and Silence
emerge from the ensemble and interact with selected people,
their presence simultaneously familiar and threatening to
Betty; their chilling response to her 'I thought you were my
friends' as she waits to be hanged is 'We are not. We are
your family' (48). These anthropomorphized personifications
contrast with the production's celebrated clog dancing ('real
dancing competitions on stage, unremitting challenges between
two performers every night in dazzling turns of nifty footwork
which were always spontaneous, never choreographed') and
live music, burning of peat, rickety wooden structures and
eighteenth-century costumes (Reade 1991: 35–6). By evoking
the music, dialect and stories of rural western Ireland, but
continually stepping out of the play's *locus* in favour of the
abstracted, theatrical spaces of classical theatre, the play both
is and is not Irish.

The play also has its Shakespearean aspects. Towards the
end of the first half of *Lady Betty*, a new character, O'Leary,
bursts onto the stage:

Arrah! Jesus, Mary and Joseph, clear the stage. Ladies and gentlemen, let's have a look at yez. Isn't it a terrible thing to fight your way to the theatre of a night and have to put up with the likes of this. All this suffering and screaming. And sure you all trying to hold down your wretched little jobs, and hoping you catch the last bus home, and coming to the theatre in the hope of a little cheer to get yez through the rest of your miserable week and what do you get but grunting and groaning. I can hear yez all saying 'O'Leary' will you entertain us in the name of all that's holy and give us a little ember to light us through the dark of our working lives. And O'Leary will oblige. O'Leary always obliges. Here now is a jolly little song from the Emerald Isle to give yez a secret little smile as yez lean over your computer keyboards tomorrow.

'Did you ever see an Irishman wear a funny hat?
Did you ever see an Irish man go rat-tat-tat?
Did you ever see an Irishman fall down flat?
No! You've never seen an Irishman do anything like that.
De deedle de deedle de deedle dee dee.'

How's that for the crack? And nothing political in it, as God is my witness. (29–30)

O'Leary is the most obviously Shakespearean element in *Lady Betty*, and Shakespearean with a particularly Cheek by Jowl stamp; his interruption references that of Anne White's Porter in the company's recent *Macbeth* (1987), with her political swipes and colourful language: 'Fuck off! Here's a fucking knocking, indeed! If youz Porter of fucking Hell Gate, you should grow old turning the fucking key' (Prescott 2008: 81). The Porter was similarly distinctive in Kelly Hotten's performance of the role in the 2009–11 production, and it is worth pausing over how Donnellan reworks the figure in his own play.

The anarchic, metatheatrical interrupter is a recurring figure in Cheek by Jowl's work. Other recurrences of this type include Prospero's shutting down of the performance in the Russian *Tempest* (see Chapter 4) and, pertinent to this chapter, the scene-stealing Autolycus of *The Winter's Tale*. O'Leary's relationship to the Porter is more pointed, however, 'deliberately drawing attention to our patronising, leprechaunish identification of the charming Irish' (Reade 1991: 36–7). O'Leary appears, as does the Porter, at a transitional moment in the play; where the Porter heralds the discovery of Duncan's murdered body and the changing of the political status quo, O'Leary marks *Lady Betty*'s relocation to Roscommon Jail. But both figures also occupy a liminal position in time and place. Both the 1987 and the 2009–11 Porters made satirical, political jokes related to their time and place: Milton Shulman referred to 'a female porter shouting expletives about stock-brokers and Tory Health Ministers' (1987). In *Lady Betty*, the Porter is reinvented as an em-cee, the fixer of the Jail and a personification of Irish craic – or Irish baloney. The device calls to mind the racist choric comedian of Christina Reid's near-contemporary *Did You Hear the One about the Irishman?* (1989), whose relentless riffs on Irish jokes descend eventually into incitements of violence. O'Leary is genial; he is not anti-Irish but, rather, wields his Irishness – dialect, song, craic – as a way of disarming the bourgeois audience who he welcomes into his prison. Cunneen's music – absent, of course, from the script – is essential to the full effect here, evoking and trivializing the stereotypes that are O'Leary's weapons, and it carries the façade of simplicity that makes the song a double-edged sword.

O'Leary, like the Porter, bridges this world and the next:

O'LEARY
　I'll bring you over the opium later.
PRISONER
　I'll pray for you in heaven.
O'LEARY
　I don't mind if you pray for me in hell. Himself has big
　　ears. (31)

Both the Porter and O'Leary guard the gateway to hell, becoming liminal figures that position the protagonist's fall at the meeting place between the everyday and the profound, reality and the afterlife, eighteenth-century Ireland and the present-day theatre. O'Leary's presence here is indicative of the importance Cheek by Jowl places on the mediating figure who demands the audience's full attention and prompts the audience to become aware of itself. O'Leary's own emphasis on the 'crack' [sic] is an important indicator of what Donnellan and Ormerod seek to achieve through these liminal figures' insistence on the theatrical present-ness of the performance.

The interplay between localized place and ¹abstracted chorus, sensory realism and liminal mediators, characterizes Cheek by Jowl productions and is embedded at the level of script in *Lady Betty*. The play is Irish, and yet it transcends location to speak to larger truths about isolation, fear and loss, as Betty moves from victim to legend. *The Winter's Tale*, similarly, used Ireland figuratively in service of discovering the value of repression, loss and family to the fourth act of the play. The fluidity of space and location will be a recurring theme throughout this book, both helping actors find the life in a given moment and simultaneously liberating them from the constraints of theatrical naturalism. In both script and rehearsal, Cheek by Jowl's practice focuses on getting to the stakes and freeing the actors to discover something genuinely alive.

2

Touching the void: bodies and space

Macbeth (2009–11) and *The Duchess of Malfi* (1995–6)

Something comes from nothing. There's nothing there, it's just us, and then we build from there up. And it's also a pledge that the imagination is going to work here. Because we haven't got anything, we're just bodies, and we stand in space, and we're going to try and make something happen. (Hille 2016)

It is not uncommon for Cheek by Jowl productions to begin by bringing the whole ensemble onto a bare stage together, offering the 'pledge' that Anastasia Hille refers to in the quotation above. In both *Macbeth* and *The Duchess of Malfi*, as well as *Twelfth Night* and *As You Like It* (Chapter 3) and many more, the company began the production by presenting themselves onstage, often wearing relatively homogeneous costumes: 'The actors are neither in nor out of character but in a limbo. This gentle confrontation locates the labour and the pleasure of the evening to come in the actors' bodies, presence and their attentiveness to us, their audience' (Prescott 2008: 76–7). In foregrounding the whole ensemble, Cheek by Jowl makes a strong statement about the role of the actor and the prioritization of the body. In Ormerod's words, 'We're saying what is the truth, which is that these are actors who are acting a story' (Reade 1991: 32). As the play begins, the actors begin to disperse, take on different identities and interact with one another, but the craft of the actor transforming their appearance is foregrounded (and indeed, in some productions, such as *Measure for Measure* (Chapter 6), the ensemble rarely left the stage).

Cheek by Jowl's emphasis on actors rather than setting lends itself to an immediate and explicit version of storytelling that begins by identifying who is present. In *The Duchess of Malfi*, the production that Roberta Barker identifies as marking the shift in the play's performance history from 'Renaissance realist' to 'modern cinematic' (Barker 2011: 54), the actors began grouped around the stage, all standing separately and facing different directions. Costume implied character, but the actors themselves stayed completely still, only coming alive as they either spoke or were spoken about. The production enacted a gradual winding up, introducing each character one at a time and quickening into motion. The effect of such strategies is to insist on the implications of action for *everyone* in the play. Where Shakespeare and his contemporaries often began plays with only two or three people onstage (Holland 2012: 16), the decision to foreground the whole company insisted on a collective investment. In these two productions of Jacobean tragedies, further, the 'expressive minimalism' (Rutter 2005: 347) of Ormerod's design and the careful management of the space between actors' bodies both emphasized the importance of those bodies and used the space between to create powerful dynamics of movement and proximity that shaped Cheek by Jowl's storytelling. The relationship between bodies and space is the subject of this chapter.

The proxemics of the Macbeths

'This is an archetypal Cheek by Jowl production: spare, disciplined, purged of gore and gratuitous spectacle,' wrote Michael Billington of *Macbeth* when it reached London in 2010.

> But, while it reflects the taste and style of Declan Donnellan and designer Nick Ormerod, and exemplifies Macbeth's desire to 'cut short all intermission', it lacks the tonal variety and narrative suspense that directors such as Rupert Goold and Greg Doran have lately brought to the play ... I don't doubt the company's talent: I just feel that they, as much as Donnellan and Ormerod themselves, are imprisoned within Cheek by Jowl's house style. (Billington 2010)

The assumptions underpinning Billington's remarks are revealing, and offer a leaping-off point for considering what Cheek by Jowl's 'house style' might be. He appeals to the memory of two recent productions that placed a great deal of emphasis on visual detail, *mise en scène* and filling the stage with *stuff*, and contrasts this with Cheek by Jowl's work, which is negatively coded in words such as 'spare,' 'purged,' 'lacks' and, later in the review, 'absence,' 'invisible' and 'cancels'. Billington casts the production as so much negative space, devoid of what previous *Macbeth*s have led him to expect.

To view Cheek by Jowl's work this way, however, is to look at Rubin's vase and only see two faces. Cheek by Jowl don't strip away; they start with a blank canvas and build up. If *Macbeth* was archetypal, it was not because it looked like a Cheek by Jowl production but because it was the epitome of a process that only uses what it needs. Contrary to the tone of Billington's remarks, Cheek by Jowl's *Macbeth* featured a very full stage; the production's emotional richness and human complexity were located in the space *between* actors, and the precise and fluid dynamics of this between-space left no room for superfluous objects, distractingly colourful costumes or conceptual gimmicks. In what follows, I aim to give a sense of how the relationship between bodies and this supposedly empty space created a *Macbeth* unlike any other.

For *Macbeth*, Donnellan and Ormerod went further than usual in avoiding the superfluous by eschewing even hand-held props. Played through in two hours without an interval, this brutally taut production organized its space around the two lead figures; as Steve Mentz notes, the 'intensity of their relationship seemed to fill up the empty space of all the things the production left out: not just elaborate politico-historical conceits such as those of Rupert Goold's faux-Soviet production with Patrick Stewart in 2009, but also visible blood, daggers, and even Weird Sisters' (2011: 622). The descent of the Macbeths into desperation was made even more stark by spatial relationships that marooned them in unrelenting darkness, placing emphasis on the precise nature of their moments of contact, distance from those they appealed to or attacked and their connection to one another. By concentrating so unflinchingly on the bodies of the actors, Donnellan and Ormerod situated *Macbeth* within a psychic environment that charted a complex series of motivations, focuses and concerns for the Macbeths.

The partnership between Will Keen (Macbeth) and Anastasia Hille (Lady Macbeth) was worked out through their physical relationship to one another, and in this section I take a single performance of 1.5.54–73 as representative of the communicative strategy developed for this production. It is important to note that, even though I go into detail here, these movements were not choreographed. As Owen Horsley puts it, in Cheek by Jowl productions, 'you're allowed, and encouraged, to keep seeing and re-seeing, and shifting and changing within a structure' (2016). The actor is not playing to hit particular points, but to respond in the living moment to what Donnellan refers to as the 'predicament' of the scene (2018). In any given performance, as each participant in a scene reacts to changing stakes, their partners in the scene need to respond in turn, meaning that the precise movements remain fluid; one of Jane Gibson's most important roles with the company, in her own terms, is to remind actors 'just to be alive in the space' (2016). The exact movements thus inevitably change nightly over a production's run. Nonetheless, the performance selected for analysis here gives a sense of how the physical work developed in rehearsal created a physical language to complement the lexical content of the scene.[1] In this sequence, the stakes could not be higher – while the overt plot has Lady Macbeth seeding the idea of assassinating Duncan, what is at stake for one another is their marriage; or, in the dual terms preferred by Donnellan, whether the two will *lose* one another or *not lose* one another. The actors' bodies in this sequence performed these stakes, creating a push/pull negotiation that I break down line by line.

Enter MACBETH	Lady Macbeth completes her soliloquy, looking to the sky and clutching her hands. Macbeth emerges from the shadows and walks purposefully towards her, but she is unaware of his presence until he reaches her. He holds out his arms at waist height, moving in for an embrace. She cries, 'Oh!' as she sees him, and her lower half jerks away from him in surprise, but she immediately puts her arms around his neck, her hands on the back of his head. He has his arms around her back. They kiss and clasp their hands, keeping their heads close together but facing one another, eye contact being essential to their intimacy throughout the scene. Throughout this they do not stop moving – the momentum of Macbeth's approach begins a spin.

Lady Macbeth: **Great Glamis!** **worthy Cawdor!**	There is a false start; they kiss after 'Great' and Lady Macbeth then repeats the word. She takes control of their turn, pulling him around, and they complete a 180-degree turn by the time she finishes 'Glamis.' She pauses, beaming, and steps away from Macbeth while holding one hand. She keeps turning, and completes another half-turn while finishing the line, now holding both his hands. On 'Cawdor,' though, Macbeth becomes uncomfortable. He shifts his hand, loosening their connection, opens his mouth and laughs loudly. She spins him another full turn and a half.
Greater than both, by the all-hail hereafter!	On conclusion of the last half-turn, Lady Macbeth pushes away and puts substantial distance between them, using verbal markers ('Nay, nay') to mark her steps as they separate. She points back at him on the emphatic 'Greater.' As she completes this sentence, he begins walking towards her, putting up his hands towards her face in an ambivalent gesture; this sequence is still a welcome home, the two desperate for physical contact, but she is also now on dangerous ground, and the hands towards her face imply restraint or silencing. She responds by reaching out her arms at waist height, preserving distance between them so she can continue speaking. She moves around him again, holding out one arm to keep a firm distance as she communicates a more dangerous idea.
Thy letters have transported me beyond	She keeps a large space between them. On 'transported me beyond', she sharply swipes her arms to both sides simultaneously, a gesture of firmness. Macbeth momentarily sits down, overpowered.

This ignorant present, and I feel now / The future in the instant.	She walks back towards him, punctuating 'future' with a downward jab of one hand. As she reaches Macbeth on 'instant', she holds out her hands towards his head to rejoin the close embrace they had earlier, but he stands again and puts his arms around her rather more forcefully.
MACBETH: My dearest love.	Macbeth pushes her backwards as he speaks, his hands firmly round her neck as he kisses her. The shift to the neck rather than the head or shoulders is a forceful, aggressive hold, taking control of the conversation again. He recognizes the danger of their conversation, and his actions simultaneously attempt to end it and to return to their interrupted reunion. As he prepares to speak again, he creates space between them by pushing away against her neck with his hand. He withdraws, his brows furrowed and hands distracted.
Duncan comes here to-night.	Macbeth holds one hand forwards in a defensive gesture, flat palm facing downwards. He uses his hand to punctuate the gravity of his words, pausing slightly before tonight and pushing down. The emphasis is clear that what he describes is immediate, serious; she steps further away.
LADY MACBETH: And when goes hence? MACBETH: To-morrow, as he purposes.	Macbeth starts stepping slowly forwards towards her, but he keeps his hand down at stomach level, flat, cautious, using the gesture to retain a visual reminder of the severity of his last statement.

Lady Macbeth: O, never / Shall sun that morrow see!	Macbeth has withdrawn, but as Lady Macbeth speaks, he moves towards her again. His ambivalence is expressed in his body moving in several directions simultaneously: his body is tilted away from her and his head is angled. He opens his mouth and holds up his hand defensively in the earlier dual-purpose silencing/embracing intention. As they meet, she now resists his attempted embrace by putting out her hand flat on his chest. She maintains arms-length distance between them, forcing him to keep his face fixed on hers and to allow her to finish speaking.
Your face, my thane, is as a book where men	She pushes him backwards, her right hand holding his left, then steps away to speak while still holding his hand. She fixes, appropriately, on his face. After 'book', she lets go of his hand and moves away, then begins walking in a long arc around him, making him turn.
May read strange matters. To beguile the time,	She completes another 180 degrees, and her elliptical orbit passes close enough to him that she can touch him on the chest on 'beguile', adding extra significance to the word. He keeps turning to follow her.
Look like the time; bear welcome in your eye,	During the first clause, she brushes hair away from her face, maintaining her focus and delivery. She puts her hand out towards him again, still maintaining the distance.
Your hand, your tongue: look like the innocent flower,	Having completed her circle, she now steps further back across the stage, holding her arms out wide as she performs her imagined welcome of Duncan. By stepping back she lets him see the full range of her body, the Duncan's-eye view of the welcoming hostess. He is rapt and holds his head in his hands. Beginning the second clause, she walks purposefully towards him, raises her arms and cradles his head.

But be the serpent under't. He that's coming	He does not respond to her hands – this is the most dangerous moment of physical connection between them. She pats his torso and then steps briskly back again, creating distance as her tone becomes matter-of-fact.
Must be provided for: and you shall put	She has retreated to let him see her full body while she explains her hospitality. He is too ill at ease for close contact to be effective, and her distance strategically allows him time and space to get on board. He is uncomfortable with his arms, stretching up and rubbing the back of his head hard.
This night's great business into my dispatch;	She holds out her arms wide on 'dispatch', and both begin slowly decreasing the distance between them.
Which shall to all our nights and days to come	She holds her arms out to the sides, slightly further apart than torso width, ready to be embraced. As he approaches, she steps back momentarily in a beautifully subtle performance of control – she is making the offer of physical contact but must finish speaking. She then allows him to reach her.
Give solely sovereign sway and masterdom.	She is still holding her arms out but now angled in a slightly defensive position, still insistent on finishing but only wanting to delay him (Figure 2). As she finishes, he scoops her aggressively into his arms, one hand on her back and another on her bottom in the most full body contact they have yet had, and he kisses her passionately. Macbeth's momentum puts them into a slow spin. He then attempts to retake control of the conversation, pushing her gently but firmly away, holding up his arm in acknowledgement and warning.
MACBETH: **We will speak further.**	There is a moment's pause as he speaks. She then reverses the dynamic by catching his hand; she recognizes his dismissal and so wrests his raised arm down to his side to retake control.

FIGURE 2 *Lady Macbeth (Anastasia Hille) and Macbeth (Will Keen). Photograph by Johan Persson/ArenaPAL; www.arenapal.com.*

LADY MACBETH: Only look up clear;	She presents herself square in his line of sight again, their two faces directly opposed. After the constant motion, the two are now, suddenly, very still together, allowing clarity for this final speech.
To alter favour ever is to fear:	She steps back, but the two stay together, still clasping hands. She pauses before her final line.
Leave all the rest to me.	She steps in closer to him and puts her hands onto his shoulders. She stares directly into his face, willing him to trust her. The lights fade as they continue looking into one another's faces.

What drives this very short sequence is the fluid negotiation of the space between two people 'bound to each other sexually very deeply' (Innes and Shevtsova 2013: 216). Charles Isherwood summarized the overall effect: 'When Macbeth arrives, she sets upon him like a bird pecking at feed, wheedling and needling him into pursing murderous ambitions that clearly would have remained beyond the limits of his imagination – hers too – if dark fate had not decreed otherwise' (2011). Isherwood's image is evocative, but renders the motion mono-directional. The natural tendency of *both* characters was to move together – the passion of this marriage and the long separation before this scene created a natural base-level momentum that drove the scene forward at breakneck speed. As Mentz puts it, 'Keen's contained fury and trembling hands seemed almost inexplicable in his first few scenes, but when they clutched eagerly at his wife's body in 1.5, the audience recognized what he was waiting for. It is hard to imagine an assassination plot with a more visible sexual subtext' (2011: 622). But the stakes of the scene shifted as Lady Macbeth brought up the letter, and both characters shifted their strategies in relation to the space: Macbeth moved physically closer both to maintain their embrace but also to stifle the conversation, and moved away to slow down the pace of new information; Lady Macbeth more strategically adjusted her distance from Macbeth according to what would rhetorically support the immediate point she was making. Breaking it down into such detail, of course, misrepresents the speed and spontaneity of the sequence. This was not a choreographed score but the outcome of two actors never losing sight of the stakes, the space and their predicament.

Hille describes this scene as emerging from rehearsal room exercises she undertook with Jane Gibson:

There were exercises that she would do that came from some distance and meeting a partner and breathing with them and then leaving them. These are very simple things – to share breath – that had a massive impact, that allowed you, with no words, just to have an engagement, to breathe with them and then to part. Another one was running a distance, and then being caught, and turning. It became part of the reel, and that idea of two bodies, spun. (2016)

The reel (seen in *Macbeth* at the start of the banquet scene) was one of the key reference points in rehearsal, just as *As You Like It*'s tango and *Cymbeline*'s step dance influenced those productions, and the energy and movement of the reel informed the meeting between the Macbeths (Sierz 2010: 155). But Hille's other remark is perhaps more interesting: 'The other thing, in terms of space, is "how do we get them to stay apart?" Because these characters just wanted to go like this [she claps her hands together]. They just wanted to do that, all the time' (Hille 2016). The challenge was to 'keep space', to ensure that the underpinning impulse – the need of husband and wife to touch, physically manifested by running together and spinning around – was counteracted by the specific objectives of the two actors. Donnellan notes that touch has to be earned: 'Sex is to do with overcoming a distance, so you have to make the distance in order for it to be overcome. Consequently the moment when you actually touch is really important' (Donnellan and Ormerod 2016). The space between the actors was not a vacuum but an energized, electric space of potential, the magnetic pull between two bodies trying to connect; this energy in turn energized the physical actions (such as Lady Macbeth resisting closeness in order to display her whole body to Macbeth) that derived from her pursuit of her individual goal (here, convincing Macbeth to leave the night's hospitality to her). The push/pull of negative space could almost be charted on a graph, the diminishing and increasing space corresponding to the subtle shifts in both characters' manipulation of one another; this three-dimensional, visual and physical dynamic acts as a language in itself.

Macbeth and the push/pull of bodies

The push/pull dynamic between bodies across space that animates this scene drove the whole production. From the opening image, when the ensemble stood facing the audience while the women spoke the words of 1.1, the bodies were kept carefully separate from one another. Contact between bodies was rare, precious and carefully used. The absolute lack of props drew even more attention to the work of the body; the first individual to emerge from the ensemble was the Bloodied Soldier, who ran downstage and mimed stabbing himself in the arm. Whether meant to signify cowardice or undermine his credibility, the image established a stage world in which bodies were kept separate when violence was inflicted upon them, removing those bodies even from the intimate contact of battle.

Contact outside of the two Macbeths largely occurred in two contexts: displays of masculine camaraderie and ceremonial fealty. The first physical contact in the production took place when a group of thanes ran in and hoisted Macbeth onto their shoulders to celebrate his becoming Thane of Cawdor. This contact was familiar and constant: slaps on the back, embraces, the comfort of colleagues. Surrounding Macbeth with these young, muscular men, Donnellan used touch to establish Macbeth's relative comfort with war. But the appearance of Duncan (David Collings) put a different spin on this. Following a decision taken in the 1987–8 production, Duncan was blind, 'metaphorically and literally' (Collins 2010: 63), and led onto the stage by his son and other thanes, all of whom held a hand on his arms, shoulders or back as he moved. Duncan's court was based around rituals of touch and proximity: when he named Malcolm (Orlando James) Prince of Cumberland, Malcolm embraced him around the waist, and Macbeth and others reached in to touch Duncan and then Malcolm. The ensemble repeatedly froze in these tableaux of touch, the contact emphasizing the trust that defined relations of fealty in this Scotland.

From his anointment on, Malcolm was regularly at the heart of these contact relations. His place as the focus of touch was explicitly visualized during the announcement of Duncan's death, during which (as is typical for Cheek by Jowl) Duncan emerged and stood upstage. On 'What is amiss?' (2.3.98),

Malcolm and Donalbain ran in and grabbed his hands; on 'Your royal father is murdered' (101), Duncan left the stage and the two brothers embraced, at which the rest of the ensemble – significantly excepting David Caves's Macduff – moved to lay their hands on the orphaned boys, the group 'transferring to [Malcolm] fealty in the sacred ritual of touch that had defined his (blind) father's rule' (Rutter 2011: 366). The Macbeths were at the centre of this huddle, publicly performing their grief; Macbeth was the last to leave, holding onto Malcolm until Malcolm himself fled. At this point, Macbeth inherited the ceremonial contact: on 'He is already named' (2.4.31), the thanes ran and knelt before him, all reaching to touch his hands. This time, Banquo (Ryan Kiggell) stayed aloof, another outlier who emphasized through their relative distance the intimacy of the network built up around the central figure. The speed at which Macbeth moved from the strategic, supportive touching of others to holding out his hands for others to kneel before him offered a brilliantly efficient visualization of his transformation in status.

In contrast to these moments of intimate contact, Lady Macbeth was repeatedly set up in isolation, at a distance from everyone she interacted with. This was to an extent gendered; Hille remembers discussions of the relative scarcity of women in this world, according them high value, and the contrast between the convivial, intimate masculine spaces and the isolation of Lady Macbeth and the witches was striking (Hille 2016). But more important was the degree to which contact represented trust, as made most explicit in Duncan's blindness. The meeting between Duncan and Lady Macbeth was instructive – as opposed to the close contact he enjoyed with the thanes, Lady Macbeth took Duncan's hand at arm's length and knelt before him, only their fingers touching in an indication of the rift that already existed in the premeditated murder. As Hille describes it, 'I'd sort of bleed any empathy I had for him in that hold, which is part of the action, so there was nothing of that left, and then once I'd released the hand, then we could kill him' (2016).

Against this backdrop, the push/pull dynamic of the Macbeths developed. During 1.7, the two began at far ends of the stage, she upstage near the light spilling over from the offstage banquet, he downstage. In her anger, she refused all contact between them, pulling away from his touch even while blocking his attempts to leave, 'frustrated to tears ... tired out by her efforts of persuasion' (Collins 2010: 64). Then, when she attempted to leave on 'Had I so sworn / As you' (1.7.58–9), Macbeth forced contact back on her, grabbing her from behind and carrying her downstage, touching her in a bid to soothe her. The remainder of the scene had them embracing on the floor, their hands touching each other's faces and torsos. Macbeth continued with his default gesture of defensiveness, holding up both hands, but now Lady Macbeth moved past it to touch him. A similar pattern emerged in 2.2 during Macbeth's distraction; they stood apart in their initial uncertainty, and only touched when Lady Macbeth attempted to get the daggers from him. Where normally this movement would have been about the props, their absence here meant that Lady Macbeth wrestled with Macbeth himself, going for his hands rather than the weapons; the intimacy of the touching here was an uncomfortable conflict. As the Macbeths became public figures, the tension created by their ability (or not) to touch became increasingly apparent. When they took their throne, they were welcomed by cheering and whooping, much to the laughing embarrassment of Lady Macbeth. They waltzed together, an intimate dance celebrating their coronation intended to recall recent images of the Obamas at the inauguration ball (Hille 2016). Later, at the beginning of the banquet scene, they danced a reel as one of several couples; a more energetic dance with the participants further apart from one another, whirling one another around. During the reel, Lady Macbeth was thrown to the floor, leaving her laughing with her mouth, if not her eyes.

The banquet scene marked the major turning point in Macbeth's descent, framed by moments of dramatic isolation. Act 3 Scene 3 saw Banquo stand downstage while the Macbeths and thanes listened to a violinist; they froze, and Banquo was killed by invisible hands, thrashing back and forth, then stretching his arms to the side as his head strained backwards. He collapsed, then relaxed and walked offstage before the banquet recommenced with the reel. The thanes then gathered in close proximity on a long bench, engaging in the same back-slapping that had hitherto marked their intimacy. Banquo's Ghost did not appear at first; Macbeth reacted to something invisible, and afterwards tried to reassure the thanes (and himself) by touching their faces and kissing their foreheads. But on 'Avaunt and quit my sight' (3.4.91), they scattered from him, and he thrashed on the floor as the ghost appeared and approached. Lady Macbeth laughed loudly throughout, a forced laughter that unsuccessfully tried to drown out Macbeth's noise. Eventually, she gave up and ordered the thanes out, at which point the Macbeths sat, facing each other from other ends of the bench. Alone, and in near silence, they began miming eating, 'united in their shared exhaustion' (Collins 2010: 64). By this stage, their emotional distance from one another was reflected in the charged gulf of empty space between them and in their mechanical actions (an emptiness repeated with full props in *Ubu Roi*, Chapter 5). Lady Macbeth eventually broke down, turned away and walked upstage, never re-establishing their contact.

The conclusion of 3.4 marked Macbeth's complete withdrawal from human contact, emphasized in the murder of the Macduffs. After his second encounter with the witches (represented by lights shone in his face), Macduff entered and sat on a box. Macbeth clapped him on the shoulder and summoned Lady Macduff (Kelly Hotten) and their children to sit with him in a family portrait (echoed in the opening to *The Winter's Tale*, Chapter 1). He arranged their posture and connections, as if attempting to re-establish human contact himself, but could not maintain it. Macduff remained onstage for 4.2, adding pathos as Young Macduff looked directly into his father's face while denying his mother's slanders. As with Banquo's murder, the violence was enacted remotely. The boy keeled over on the floor while Lady Macduff, her hands bound behind her, screamed. She then threw herself over a box, spread her legs and jerked, and then her neck snapped to one side, all while Macduff sat silently between his wife and son. The isolation of the victims exaggerated the detached nature of the crimes and, by having the actors enact their own rape and murder, put the management of those fates into the hands of those actors, rendering Macduff helpless. As Hille puts it, 'you're allowed into the middle ground of that intimacy, that violation' (2016). Macduff, in turn, then became the central focus of intimacy; on hearing the news of his family's slaughter, the thanes gathered around and 'braced' his shoulders and arms. As he got to his feet and roared, 'Did Heaven look on?' (4.3.226), the supportive hands became restraints, protecting him as he raged at heaven, 'otherwise he's going to take off, he's going to explode, to die' (Hille 2016). Malcolm, distanced from Macduff through his earlier acts of deception and already anticipating the civil fealty he would perform at the production's close, only took Macduff's hand. The image was one of collective empathy, with Malcolm slightly detached.

While Macduff became the centre of contact, the Macbeths continued in isolation, until the point of death. At the close of 5.1, Lady Macbeth was alone onstage, kneeling and toying with her hands, and she remained onstage as Macbeth entered with 'Bring me no more reports' (5.3.1) and came straight over to her. Throughout this scene, Macbeth never let go of Lady Macbeth, playing with her hair; in their absolute separation, she became his anchor. As he said 'I have lived long enough' (22), she smiled nervously up at him, and on 'Give me my armour' (33), she helped him take off his jacket. When, as part of the same sequence, the cry of women was heard, he looked down at Lady Macbeth and continued stroking her hair; then, on 'The Queen, my lord, is dead' (5.5.16), she pulled away and left the stage. The two remained separate until the play's final moments, when Lady Macbeth emerged from the wings to lie down next to Macbeth's body, the lights lingering on the two of them as they finally touched again in death.

Where Billington reads a lack of 'tonal variety', I read a complex and hugely varied approach to negative space as the Macbeths negotiated each other through touch and isolation. The relative starkness of this production drew attention to the proxemics of the actors' bodies, whether in intimate contact or subjected to dissociated violence, which revealed the 'dynamically opposed contradictions [that] free the actor more' (Donnellan 2005: 84). In the push and pull between bodies, the company exposed the rawness of human attempts to engage with one another amid dehumanizing acts.

The Duchess of Malfi: tableaux and diagonals

Right from its opening, the bodies of *The Duchess of Malfi* were askew. 'One aspect of the design is the exact positioning of the few elements that we use,' explains Donnellan, 'and also the shapes that the actors make across the stage, whether in diagonals or at right angles, their entrances and exits, are all part of the design. In *The Duchess of Malfi*, for example, the actors would cross the stage obliquely to the audience, which was unsettling' (Sierz 2010: 155). Hille explains further:

> The essence of the situations and the world of the play, if you like, was oblique. You never really head off [or] head on, you don't have that honest, stable relationship [where] I am open to you. I'm always going to be at a diagonal to you and the world ... I remember a lot of work moving through space, the effect of corridors, of diagonals, and individuals walking in diagonals, groups in diagonals, the energy of that – where they meet, where they don't meet. Because there's always an area of you which is hidden on a diagonal. (2016)

The precision implied here is important, particularly when Cheek by Jowl's movement is so often characterized as 'free'; indeed, Paul Prescott picks up on a line in the promptbook of *Much Ado about Nothing* (1998) that states 'Bea[trice] free to roam here' (2008: 74). Donnellan himself has elsewhere stated, 'You don't need to tell [actors] where to stand, you need to make sure that they know what's happening in the scene, and then wonderful things will happen out of the scene because none of us has overburdened it with rules' (Donnellan and Ormerod 1996: 90). This isn't the paradox it might at first seem; while Donnellan is unlikely to ever instruct an actor to sit down at a particular point, the *études* and movement work provide a framework for actors' interactions. Freedom to move within the scene is not *absolute* freedom, because the actors are trained to respond to one another according to the constraints of the stakes, the predicament and the space. In *Malfi*, the structural principle of working on diagonals was not a law but a framework within which the actors explored the kinds of interaction possible within this environment. What Hille describes as a partially 'hidden' mode of being came into its own in a production that placed bodies at uncanny and disorientating angles to one another, the off-centre sightlines and walkways creating a spatial architecture with bodies that established the production's complex dynamics of watching.

The floor of Ormerod's set evoked a chessboard, its squares angled at 45 degrees to the stage's horizontal axis. When the curtain was raised, the ensemble were revealed to be standing in isolation at various points around the stage, all facing in different directions.[2] Contrasting with the unity of the Chorus as witches at the start of *Macbeth*, *The Duchess of Malfi* established a world in which bodies were distinctly separate from one another, making even the intimacy of eye contact across the space an important marker of connection. Yet while the distribution of the bodies defied obvious structure, the diagonals of the flooring created sightlines and patterns, stressed in Judith Greenwood's lighting that emphasized the disorientated space (Greenwood 1998: 15), cutting through to provide clarity at key moments. This worked in conjunction with the company technique that Christopher Innes and Maria Shevtsova define as 'tableau-freeze ... signifying that [characters] belong to the whole story of the play' (2013: 213), which I will discuss further in Chapter 4. For much of the opening sequence, the whole company remained onstage, frozen. Those actors directly involved in the scene ricocheted between the statues, looking into the unmoving faces of those they spoke about, casting the nature of their diegetic reality into doubt.

The effect of this was to set up a world of strict hierarchies where scenes were repeatedly performed for the benefit of particular characters or centred around an unmoving figure. For much of the production, this was Hille's Duchess. Even in the opening tableau, Greenwood's lighting subtly illuminated her face where she stood centre stage, making her body a fixed point around which the other actors arranged themselves. Importantly, however, she was not in complete isolation; as Bosola, Antonio and Delio talked about them in 1.1, the figures of the Duchess, Ferdinand and the Cardinal came to life, dressed in finery by attendants and positioned in a diagonal bathed in light as a public display of their power. Roberta Barker argues that the production particularly tried to encourage identification between the Duchess and Ferdinand, this 'main interpretative thrust ... signalled for the spectator by the first pages of [the production's] programme [that] featured juxtaposed photographs of Anastasia Hille and Scott Handy, accentuating the physical resemblance of the two actors' (2007: 67). While this is true to an extent, Greenwood's yellow lighting framed all three siblings, including Paul Brennen's Cardinal, together.

Much has been written on the relative confidence and authority of Hille's Duchess, from Ben Brantley's description of her as 'the very image of tyrannical aristocratic charm ... who brandishes a cigarette like a dagger and a dagger like a cigarette' (1995) to Barker's description of her stressing 'the

Duchess' power over others ... [her] fragile elegance was contradicted by her fierce resolve' (2007: 61). This effect owed much to Donnellan and Ormerod's management of the tableau-freeze on the diagonals, which positioned Hille and, to a noticeable but lesser extent, Brennen as focal points for the scenes. Handy's Ferdinand, by contrast, was barely ever the subject of a tableau-freeze. Throughout the production, he wheeled about the stage, drawing large arcs with his body and expending frenetic energy, while the Duchess and Cardinal stood or sat calmly, poised. This relative stillness orientated the scene around them, turning them into a focal point of the scenic design and accentuating their authority.

For the Duchess in particular, this rendered the men in her life not only subordinate to her but practically childlike. When Ferdinand pulled his poniard on her (1.1.331), she took it away from him and chastened him, barely taking a break from drags on her cigarette. During her soliloquy (1.1.341ff), Ferdinand froze in a ridiculous position, his poniard thrust out in a tableau of wasteful energy, he smiling and lunging, while the Duchess walked unconcernedly around him, her aloof superiority contrasting with his ridiculousness. Handy's energy led to his repeated infantilization by the others: during 2.5, Ferdinand was positioned between a tableau of the Duchess and Antonio (the latter facing away) and the seated Cardinal, almost as still as the statue. The tableau-freeze perfectly captured Ferdinand's conception of the Duchess – fully visible to him, but with a faceless man in shadow – and allowed him to express his feeling by screaming in her face, though it was this action that prompted the Cardinal to finally get up from his chair, slap him, throw him to the floor and drag him across the stage. Later still, while intruding into her bedchamber, he put both of his legs over hers while sat with her on the floor in order to tell the story of Reputation, Love and Death (3.2.120–35), as if a child sitting on her lap. Concluding his speech with 'I will never see you more,' he covered his own eyes and tried to leave, comically stumbling over a chair on his way out.

The casting of Matthew Macfadyen, barely in his twenties and thus a decade younger than Hille, as Antonio carried this imbalance in maturity over into the Duchess's romantic relationship. In order to mitigate her superiority, she adopted a meek, quiet voice in 1.2, coaxing him into giving answers about his feelings towards her and marriage. Casting Antonio as a 'very young and desperately prim civil servant, a junior Malvolio' (Barker 2007: 71) emphasized the class inequality, but also aligned Antonio with Ferdinand as the two men besotted with but ultimately unequal to the Duchess. This was particularly clear in the push/pull of their final parting in 3.5, a desperately sad reading of the scene, in which a stand-offish Antonio was more interested in holding Bosola at gunpoint than engaging directly with the Duchess. Defaulting to her usual mode when unsettled, the Duchess stood to one side of the stage, smoking and keeping her distance. She coolly instructed Antonio to take his son and leave, and he responded crossly. The two were separated at far sides of the stage with Cariola, holding a baby and pushing a pram, dividing them. As Antonio strode off, only acknowledging Cariola, he walked past the Duchess, causing her to sob and break, clawing at and embracing him as she cried 'that speech / Came from a dying father' (3.5.85–6). But as he tried to pull her closer, she broke away and again went to the far side, causing him to resume his petulant attitude and walk off. The Duchess's relative stillness and fixity insisted that the men around her work for and towards her; the moments where she broke out of her rigidity and petitioned another were rare, but all the more powerful for that.

The shapes into which characters fell became a structural semiotic model that illustrated relative power relations as a way of indicating the primary focus for those onstage. The Duchess's stillness resonated with that of the Cardinal, although his demonstrated a more sinister power. In his opening scene with Julia, the two sat on chairs separately, she facing towards him along a diagonal and he facing away, establishing a clear visual power dynamic in which she was subservient to him.

Such simple images acted as snapshots around which the movements of a scene were orientated and established clearly who was performing for whom.

The Duchess as focal point

The second half of *The Duchess of Malfi* (4.1–5.5, following the interval) went further than any other production in justifying the play's title, with the Duchess remaining onstage for the entire sequence. Further, the diagonals of the stage worked to imply that the final two acts formed a kind of pageant performed on her behalf, her eyeline commanding the rest of the stage and establishing her as the character with the fullest understanding of the stage action, even after her death.

The stage juxtaposed two focal points from the rise of the curtain: the Duchess, framed centre stage, and a crucifix downstage, in front of which Cariola knelt praying for much of 4.1. The tension between these two focal points became explicit as the Duchess herself briefly knelt before the crucifix on 'I'll go pray,' before, in a moment of frustration, hurling it to the floor with 'No, I'll go curse' (4.1.95–6). Given the relative sparseness of the set (at this point, the busiest in the play – a bed, three chairs, a table and a candelabra) the action seemed particularly destructive, and the moment caused controversy at a performance in Malta in February 1996.

> There was this kind of gasp. There was a general feeling of people rushing to the exits, of noise and action going off. And then – I think it was the next day – there was press, the police were involved, [and] there was some sort of threat about it, because in Malta the cross is a sacred object, and it must not be touched, and certainly not kicked, in a public place … I remember there was a backlash then from the young people of Malta who then put the thing out in

the press saying 'this is an outrage, this is censorship, this is not the country we want to live in.' And there was a real outcry then, and then there was a conservative response to that – it seemed to go on for a while afterwards. (Hille 2016)[3]

While the Maltese controversy was specific to a particular context of reception, the significance of the moment lay in its disruption of the spatial focus. The initial significance placed on the crucifix by its downstage positioning was misleading, and the crucifix was rendered increasingly impotent throughout the scene; while early on the Cariola/crucifix tableau provided a fixed point against which the Duchess's nervous drinking, smoking and pacing could be measured, increasingly the crucifix became obviously impotent, with Cariola clinging onto it desperately as events spiralled out of control, while the Duchess became more composed, more measured. The Duchess's violent act was an important visual signifier of her insisting on her own importance as the scene's focus and establishing her right to self-determination; the physical equivalent of her line, 'I am Duchess of Malfi still' (4.2.137).

In the first half of the production, a repeated staging motif saw the Duchess sat in a chair, isolated, while a group of attendants arranged in a diagonal line faced her. This arrangement was parodied and inverted by the arrival of the madmen, who arranged themselves before her to perform a pageant that included a large-breasted queen (Peter Moreton) who gave birth in comic, grotesque manner to a doll that he then nursed before being forced to give it up. The parody of the Duchess's situation was a cruel mockery of their audience. The madmen were replaced by attendants, and the preparations for her murder saw her take her position of authority centre stage while the men surrounded her from a distance. The men closed in on her, concealed her from view while (apparently) pulling a rope tight around her neck, and then stepped away, lowering her to a lying position.

Downstage and diagonally opposite her, the same happened to Cariola, only with Cariola thrashing and left splayed in contrast to the perfectly straight, posed body of the Duchess, their feet towards one another.

The diagonal pattern created by the two bodies – the Duchess with head pointed towards upstage right, Cariola with head pointed towards downstage left – became the primary axis for everything that ensued. As Bosola and Ferdinand feuded over the Duchess's body, they positioned themselves perpendicular to the axis created by the women's bodies, separated by that imaginary line. As the scene ended and the stage was bathed in green, the Duchess and Cariola got up and walked along their diagonal to upstage right, where Cariola left the stage and the Duchess sat on a chair in front of the candelabra. While Ferdinand thrashed on the floor, entering into his lycanthropic state, the Duchess's illuminated face stared directly down her diagonal, as if the remaining scenes were another performance for her benefit. During 5.2, the Cardinal took up his usual centre-stage position, this time standing with his hand on the back of a chair, while Ferdinand chased a group of doctors in large circles around the stage; the overt performance of the scene for the Cardinal's benefit became a subsidiary performance, with the Cardinal dead centre in the Duchess's eyeline. This meant she also had a perfect view of the Cardinal's interrogation of Bosola, and of Julia and Bosola's plot. This last was particularly important, as it took place entirely on the Duchess's diagonal, with Julia centre stage and Bosola standing downstage left, looking directly at Julia, but also past her at the Duchess.

The use of this striking upstage-right/downstage-left diagonal created a spatial alleyway marked only by the direction in which the Duchess was looking, but that organized everyone else's blocking. The Cardinal's murder of Julia took place in this alleyway, as did the Echo scene (5.3). Antonio and Delio stood centre stage facing downstage left, with the Duchess moving her head to watch Antonio as he paced. As

Hille spoke the echoes, she stood up behind Antonio and then moved forwards along the diagonal as she spoke, staying within the alley and coming slowly to life with increased volume and expression, embodying Susan Anderson's note aligning the corporeality of echoic figures with their ability to articulate (2018: 56). When she reached 'Thou art a dead thing!' (5.3.38), she shouted, even reaching her hand momentarily towards him, before her voice broke on 'Never see thee more' (41), at which she turned around and walked back to her chair, resuming her still position. Here, the brief shift from her position of watcher to the haunting possibility of momentary resurrection reinforced the importance of her position of oversight and allowed for the pathos-laden evocation of near-contact, the two close together once again but never meeting one another's eyes. From her seated position on the stage, she watched the Cardinal, Ferdinand, Bosola and Antonio die, spread around the stage and stabbing one another virtually, the distance between the actors serving (as in *Macbeth*) as a reminder of psychic separation, as mistaken identities and distorted minds accelerated the slaughter. As he stabbed out blindly, Bosola positioned himself at a right angle to the Duchess's diagonal, the thrusts of swords cutting across her line of sight.

As Roberta Barker argues, Cheek by Jowl's production 'depicted a Duchess who found herself completely isolated, who desired death but who could not move those around her to end her life' (2007: 74). The spatial isolation of the Duchess throughout the production, drawing on her stability in order to render the men of her world subservient to her across the perverted angles of Ormerod's stage, used the empty space to construct the Duchess herself as the most important piece of scenery, her movements and positions dictating what was possible for others. Despite her murder, her presence in tableau insisted on a reading of the story as that of the Duchess, her presence (real or projected) rendered continuously physical in order to cast everyone's actions as done for her.

Conclusion

The target is not how we see things. The target is what we see. The split target is the stakes. At every living moment there must be something to be lost and something to be won (Donnellan 2005: 59).

The most significant governing principle of Donnellan and Ormerod's work insists on the identification of the external object of the actor's action. In the two case studies of this chapter, I have shown how the 'spare, disciplined' house style of Cheek by Jowl is far from being 'empty space'; rather, this space energizes the proxemics of the stage that physicalize what is at stake. The use of the tableau-freeze, the interplay of motion and stillness and the separation of individual bodies all serve to concentrate and focalize interpretive energy on the precise movements and potential energy of the actor's body. By continually displaying and foregrounding bodies that are spoken about, as well as those that are speaking, Donnellan and Ormerod visualize and physicalize each moment, helping the actors to see what is at stake.

While Cheek by Jowl's work is rarely as spare and unrelenting as in these two tragedies, the relationships between body and space inform all of the company's productions. By abstracting actors from the conventions and restrictions of the imagined location of scenes, the space between actors comes into play as a series of fluctuating, carefully managed forces that respond intuitively to the diegetic and psychic needs of the scene. In a Cheek by Jowl production, a character can be alone within a crowd, intimate from a great distance or the focal point of a scene that they aren't in. The storytelling takes place in the space between those actors' bodies, a space that may be unpopulated, but never empty.

3

'If I were a woman': the all-male ensemble

Twelfth Night (2003–) and *As You Like It* (1991–5)

An occasional misapprehension of Cheek by Jowl is the emphasis on them as an 'all-male company', such as in Terri Power's grouping of the company with Propeller and the Lord Chamberlain's Men (2016: 68). Power's grouping of Cheek by Jowl with these other companies implies that the company's core practice is single-gendered, which is perhaps a result of two of the company's most successful productions having all-male companies – the acclaimed *As You Like It* that toured internationally in two separate versions between 1991 and 1995; and *Twelfth Night*, one of the company's longest-running productions that has remained almost continuously in the repertory in Russia (as well as on international tours) since 2003. Power's listing of Cheek by Jowl among the all-male companies whose 'formation and prosperity' has benefitted from all-male experiments at Shakespeare's Globe does Cheek by Jowl a further disservice by eliding the fact that Cheek by Jowl got there first by half a decade.[1]

Cheek by Jowl was far from the first company to experiment with all-male casting. Chad Allen Thomas notes that the Glasgow Citizen's Theatre in the 1970s was one of the first to innovate with cross-dressing and queer politics (2010: 104), and Robert Shaughnessy discusses at some length the National's 1967 all-male production of *As You Like It* (2017: 162), though James Bulman argues that the latter was an 'isolated experiment', occurring at a time 'when audiences were not yet ready seriously to entertain questions of gender construction and when representations of homosexuality were still banned from the British stage' (2008: 90). The influence of Cheek by Jowl's two productions, including on the two younger all-male companies, has had lasting ramifications; *As You Like It* in particular has inspired more scholarly articles than the rest of the company's output combined, and *Twelfth Night*, the company's contribution to the RSC's Complete Works Festival in 2007 and its longest-running Shakespeare production, has also been widely seen and discussed, particularly in the context of queered approaches to Shakespeare performance.

In this chapter, I continue the previous chapter's focus on bodies, but in discussion of these two productions of comedies, I attend more closely to the ensemble. Where *Macbeth* and *The Duchess of Malfi* used empty space to draw attention to the proxemics of bodies, *Twelfth Night* and *As You Like It* allow for detailed study of the company's construction of 'fundamentally performative' identities (Shaughnessy 2017: 180). Both productions can be read through a queer lens, and the productions' serious presentation of male–male relationships (both between actors playing differently gendered characters and between male characters) has been significant to queer theorists of Shakespeare, but I would argue that the most important feature of these productions in this regard was the naturalistic acting that treated the love relationships as *unexceptional*; there was nothing arch, caricatured or broad about the performances. Both productions foregrounded the gender presentation of the actors in the ensemble as male, but neither exaggerated nor attempted to hide that maleness even as the actors dressed as women; Donnellan 'had a missionary zeal to avoid the British pantomime tradition or to fall into that more ... Mediterranean sort of *travestie*' (Donnellan 2003: 164). In many respects, these productions were no different in their approach to anything else in Cheek by Jowl's repertoire: *Vanity Fair* (1983–5), for instance, had had seven actors play over forty roles of both male and female genders (as well as two dogs), with Donnellan noting that 'theatrical lying is vitally important because it's through that that we can tell each other the truth' (Reade 1991: 32). The company has always acknowledged the craft of the actor as storyteller, and in casting an all-male company for *As You Like It*, Cheek by Jowl had 'no interpretative view of it other than ... to start with that as something to be investigated' (Reade 1991: 95), adopting something of the play's own self-conscious gender games. The choice to cast only men was a rare pre-rehearsal choice for the company, but was designed to open up new options, rather than commit to a particular reading. In pairing the productions here, therefore, I am less concerned with exploring the specifics of the productions' queerness than with considering how the explicit exposure of identity construction in both productions speaks to Cheek by Jowl's work with the actor on the development of character as both an individual and an ensemble phenomenon.

Forming identities in *Twelfth Night*

The company's attention settles on a slight, brown-haired young man (Andrei Kuzitchev [*sic*]). Two actors pull the young man forward and wrap him in a skirt. Kuzitchev blinks, then giggles and covers his mouth with both hands as if to ask, 'Are you serious?' The skirt and giggle might otherwise seem a clichéd performance of gender, except that Kuzitchev next scans the stage, looking intently to his colleagues, who do not react negatively, before he accepts his role (Viola) with a shrug of his shoulders and crosses off-stage. With his shrug, Kuzitchev suggests that playing a female role is no big deal, and he accepts Viola ... Yet when Kuzitchev moves, a gendered difference is immediately noticeable from his initial march around the stage: instead of heavy clomping, he skips lightly away. The boundaries between male and female are so porous that the addition of a skirt is all a Cheek by Jowl actor needs to become a female character. (Thomas 2010: 107)

The playful opening of *Twelfth Night* brought on a group of actors wearing identical white shirts, dark trousers and braces.[2] As opposed to the separation that characterized the opening sequences of *Macbeth* and *The Duchess of Malfi*, however, the whole ensemble here worked together, acknowledging and then dressing one of their own. Importantly, the skirt that Thomas notes in his description above was in fact not Viola's costume; when he re-entered a scene later, Kuzichev wore a full dress. The handing over of the skirt, therefore, was symbolic, even ritualistic. The moment was preceded by several of the men speaking the words 'My father' until Viola completed the phrase 'My father was of Messaline / He left behind a daughter' (2.1.16–18).[3] The game here implied that any of these identically dressed men *could* have become that daughter, and it was Kuzichev's words that produced him as Viola.

The entry of the company together draws attention to the unusual (by Western standards) ensemble nature of the Russian company, with actors working together in repertoire for life; as Alexander Feklistov puts it, 'an actor basically auditions once in a lifetime when he is showing himself to different theatre companies after graduation' (2016). After directing *The Winter's Tale* for the Maly in 1997 at the invitation of Lev Dodin, Donnellan and Ormerod were invited by the Chekhov

International Theatre Festival to form their own company of Russian actors in Moscow in 1999, and Maria Shevtsova calls Donnellan 'the only director in Britain to have a consistent working relationship with Russia' (Donnellan 2009: 66). For *Boris Godunov* (2000–), a play written in conscious imitation of Shakespeare, the company assembled an all-star ensemble drawn from various companies for a shockingly 'contemporary' yet 'mythic' (Brantley 2009) version of Russian history that won over audiences who had questioned, 'How can a foreigner understand the Russian soul?' (Donnellan 2009: 81). *Boris Godunov* combined 'breathtaking ensemble performance, sharp anachronisms (Godunov dressed like President Putin juxtaposed against archaic monks) and an equally pointed connection between the political–ethical dilemmas addressed by Pushkin and those confronting post-communist Russia' (Shevtsova 2005: 236). The ensemble came in for particular attention in the reviews; as Anya Kolesnikova notes, this 'was one of the very first occasions when people from different theatre companies were brought together on one project' (Kolesnikova 2016). The next two productions, *Twelfth Night* (2003–) and *Three Sisters* (2005–), were developed with the same ensemble, allowing Donnellan to develop long-term relationships with actors: 'What I really like about Russians is the attention that they pay each other ... They're attentive to each other, not in a particularly intense, but often in a sort of lightly worn and human way ... I am a big one for continuity in my life and the *actor* continuity in my life is exclusively Russian' (Donnellan 2009: 80–1). This long-term commitment also informs Donnellan and Ormerod's work on their French productions (see Chapter 5). The trust and community acknowledged at the opening of *Twelfth Night* is endemic to the Russian company's work.

The speed and ease of Kuzichev's transition to Viola set up the ensemble's approach to the social construction of gender, fluid and produced discursively in line with attitudes to gender within the play. After Viola left the stage, Vladimir Vdovichenkov also produced a woman, but this time from another actor. As Orsino, Vdovichenkov spoke, 'O, when mine eyes did see Olivia first' (1.1.18), at which Alexey Dadonov stepped forward. Orsino himself put the skirt around Dadonov's waist, then stepped back to admire the statuesque tableau of a woman he had created, walking around the edges of the stage to appraise her. Gender was not just self-determined but constructed by others, with Olivia constructed from the start as an object of Orsino's gaze. Gendered identity did not exist in isolation but in relation to other members of the ensemble.

The production further complicated and queered its gender presentations as more figures appeared. Ilya Ilyin appeared unambiguously in a dress as Maria, but Igor Yasulovich was less initially clear, appearing first in a long coat and hat, his camp stance and swaying hips muddying distinctions between him and Maria. In taking off his hat, he revealed a balding patch, and on removing his coat he was revealed to be wearing a suit with an over-large jacket. Yasulovich's gender-fluid, gay Feste was joined by Antonio (Mikhail Zhigalov, burly and aggressive in shirt sleeves and jacket), Malvolio (Dmitry Shcherbina, in full suit and tails, but later a straitjacket that fell about his waist like a skirt), Sir Andrew (standing with performative bravado) and Orsino himself, who for many of his scenes wore a long dressing gown that lent him a feminized appearance, before he assumed a full suit and square-shouldered stance for the final scene. Gender performance was, therefore, not simply binary; the naturalistic, elegant movements of the three actors playing women certainly distinguished them as women, but the contrasting impressions of masculinity (including Kuzichev's Cesario) were multifaceted and complex, showcasing a broad spectrum of masculine identities, in what Paul Edmondson describes as a 'lyricism of gender' (2007: 81).

The variety in ideas about masculinity within the production did the important work of avoiding a default or baseline maleness from which the men-as-women deviated, illustrating perfectly Terri Power's point that:

In our male-centric society masculinity is seen as the one 'true' gender' [*sic*] (the rest are 'other' or non-genders) and establishes its dominance as natural through appropriation of mostly unnatural signs. Through closer observation, these 'natural' characteristics are found to be infinite in expression as no two masculinities are alike. (2016: 23)

In starting from a shared blank template and layering the characters with different, individualized versions of masculinity and femininity, Cheek by Jowl offered a version of gender that treated maleness as being as much of a construction as femaleness. The clearest example of this came in the duel between Viola and Andrew. Toby and Feste stage-managed the arena, placing chairs in opposite corners of the stage, as if preparing a boxing ring. Kuzichev's Viola crouched on top of her chair, terrified, while Andrew entered in full boxing regalia including bright red shorts, helmet and kneepads, punching the air in a performance of violence; yet on seeing Viola, he too cowered. As Viola said, 'A little thing would make me tell them how much I lack of a man' (3.4.295–6), Andrew peered into his shorts, as if checking to see if his penis was still there. The juxtaposition of words and action applied the line to both characters in a metatheatrical acknowledgement of the actors' shared biology; Andrew/Yasulovich lacked precisely as much of manhood as did Viola/Kuzichev, and masculinity was indistinguishable from performance. Andrew's inability to perform meant his masculinity collapsed under the slightest scrutiny, but in performing this moment of emasculation he drew attention back to the underpinning male bodies that he and Kuzichev shared. If Kuzichev was a man playing a woman playing a man, Yasulovich was a man playing a man playing at being 'a man'.

The playful fluidity of the production aligned with the play's own, drawing comedy from group performance. During Cesario's first embassy to Olivia (1.5), both Maria and Feste donned veils along with their mistress, and the three 'women' circled a disconcerted Viola. Whereas most productions make

Viola mobile among statuesque veiled figures, the choice to have the veiled figures in motion allowed the performatively female household to literally run rings around the performatively male interloper. When all three figures unveiled simultaneously, re-producing their primary identities, the servants fled the stage; yet as they did so, Feste took a moment to cheekily touch Viola's bottom: a gay character presenting as male touching a male actor playing a woman presenting as male. Feste's brief objectification of Cesario set the stage for Olivia's more sustained sexual interest in him, but also queered Kuzichev/Viola/Cesario's body, establishing the male body (Kuzichev/Cesario) as a passive recipient of unwanted sexual attention. Yet within the play's diegesis, this was simultaneously a dirty old man groping a young woman. Viola's entrance into Olivia's household thus did triple work: it set up the character as an object of sexual interest; it identified the male body of the actor as passive; and it established a world that threw out easy distinctions between performatively masculine and performatively feminine behaviours.

The indistinguishability of the three veiled figures was an affordance of the all-male ensemble, in which gender and social identity were simply matters of donning costume; to all intents and purposes, the actors *were* veiled Olivias so long as they chose to be and were read as such by Viola. This is, of course, the same imaginative logic that successful productions of *Twelfth Night* have always exploited, in which 'we are persuaded to see a boy in boy's clothes as a woman ... we *imagine* her into being' (Brown 2014: 301). The indistinguishability of Cesario and Sebastian (Evgeny Tsyganov), as usual, involved the two actors wearing identical costumes that led them to be read as one body. But Donnellan and Ormerod's preference for overlapping scene transitions (see Chapter 4) exploited this further by repeatedly juxtaposing the visual appearance of Sebastian with words describing Viola. At the end of 1.5, Olivia moved downstage to discuss Cesario, at which point Sebastian appeared upstage right, bathed in light. Judith Greenwood's lighting design here transferred Olivia's mental idealization of Cesario *onto* Sebastian. The company's standard convention of visualizing characters who are spoken about but not literally present here prefigured Olivia's eventual pairing with Sebastian, and also showed the arbitrariness of Olivia's infatuation, slipping indiscriminately between brother and sister. The production continued to overlap the two characters, allowing Olivia's 'I have sent after him' (3.4.1) to interrupt just before Sebastian's 'I'll be your purse bearer' (3.3.47), again juxtaposing their bodies onstage. Once they had met, Sebastian's version of masculinity was directly contrasted with Andrew's: Andrew knocked Sebastian's hat off and pushed him, at which Sebastian (after gently adjusting his outfit) punched Andrew full in the face. With the rivals beaten, Sebastian kissed Olivia and left willingly with her, and was next seen in only his underpants, throwing his clothes joyfully into the air. Cheek by Jowl frequently displays exposed bodies at points of truth and vulnerability, and Sebastian's exposure at the point of the production's purest expression of ecstatic love was no accident, throwing away all distinguishing markers of gender and status.[4] Only when Olivia appeared in a wedding dress did Tsyganov resume the clothes that rendered him Sebastian.

Masculinity and disorder in *Twelfth Night*

Andrew's unsuccessful performance of manhood was just one way in which the production held up versions of masculinity for consideration and critique. Alexander Feklistov (Sir Toby) speaks of how early explorations of juxtaposing Illyria's preparations for carnival-time with the enforced mourning of Olivia's household informed his performance:

> This idea was very close to me. I grew up in a very puritan Soviet environment, where many adults drowned their incomprehension of life in vodka. As a boy I saw many

adult men in a drunken sleep outside under the fence. That happened regularly. And that was a key to start discovering Sir Toby for me. He is striving for a feast; the circumstances of life are too tight for him. His love for his niece is in conflict with unwillingness to be in mourning, to obey the order and the law. (2016)

Toby's zest for life put him into tension with the subdued household epitomized by Malvolio's straight lines and ordered tidying. To my English-attuned ear, at least, his rasping voice and blunt outbursts were aggressively joyful, a confrontation as much as a celebration. The production's defining moment came during the carousals scene (2.3), with Toby even more drunk and careless than usual. The scene saw a jolly Feste sitting on Andrew's knee and the three men singing together, then moving to dancing. Maria entered from the shadows and took Toby's drink off him, to which Toby initially reacted quietly. Then, on 'Am I not consanguineous?' (2.3.76), he punched her hard in the face, knocking her to the floor.

The moment of violence used the conventions and the tolerance afforded an all-male production to push Toby and Maria's relationship to a darker place than usual. The semiotics of a male actor punching a female actor are difficult for a production to recover from in contemporary Western theatre, and while it is depressingly common for stage productions to ramp up the graphic nature of sexual violence, such decisions are usually introduced in order to emphasize a character's villainy.[5] An all-male company, however, seems to allow (or assume) a greater level of tolerance for extreme, even cartoonish violence, a tolerance particularly exploited by Edward Hall's Propeller Theatre in their 2006–7 *The Taming of the Shrew*, which manipulated the audience into laughing in complicity at the physical violence meted out on Simon Scardifeld's Katherine before revealing the extent of her brokenness. In Cheek by Jowl's *Twelfth Night*, the punch caused an audible outcry at every performance I attended, prompted I suggest by the suddenness of the act and the gentleness of Ilyin's performance as Maria. The moment paradoxically depended on the audience simultaneously remembering and forgetting Ilyin's gender identity, the outrage mitigated by the artifice. In this doubled viewing, the audience was invited to see a relationship driven to breaking point by Toby's uncontrollable outbursts.

What followed was surprisingly beautiful. Feste helped Maria into a chair, and he and Andrew looked after her while Toby packed up the drinks in a plastic bag. Toby then staggered, turned and saw Maria sobbing quietly into her hands while nursing her bruises. He flapped his own hands around, conscious of what he had done. Then he crossed to her, leant over and buried his face in her shoulders, seemingly also crying. He began singing, quietly at first, and as he sang, Maria started singing with him, downing several shots that had been poured for her as she did so. As the song crescendoed, Maria began dancing, moving in tiny steps while waving a handkerchief. As the alcohol and communal singing dulled her pain, the men lifted her onto the kitchen table, she performing a high kick as she ascended. The production took the time to register and acknowledge the severity of Toby's actions, and used that to develop a communal expression of intimacy and forgiveness. Toby's self-destructive behaviours hurt the one closest to him, and in his grunting sobs and childlike nudging of his head against hers, he expressed a regret for which he had no words. Maria medicated through alcohol and implicitly forgave him; he responded in the play's second half with sobriety, donning a summer suit. The production didn't condone his violence; nor did his punch remove the possibility of grace. As so often with Cheek by Jowl productions, the messiness of human behaviours was laid bare rather than tidied up.

This messiness was in no-one so clear as Shcherbina's Malvolio. The officious butler first appeared in Olivia's household (1.5), trying to physically block Feste from approaching Olivia, and then taking out a handkerchief with which to pick up Feste's suitcase, avoiding touching the dirtied baggage of a man he disdained. Malvolio's superiority was expressed through his insistence on dignified self-possession, commingled with condescension. At times he took pleasure in his superiority, most notably when he 'returned' Olivia's ring to Cesario (2.2); as he faced Cesario, he raised his arm as if to throw it violently, causing Cesario to step back, cowering and raising her arms to protect herself. Malvolio smugly lowered his arm and put the ring gently on the floor, before turning and striding off. The small pleasure he took in this moment of bullying (to his knowledge between two men) was as far as Shcherbina went in demonstrating his vindictiveness.

Shcherbina's Malvolio was distinguished throughout by his restraint. The display of the yellow stockings in 3.4, so often a set piece that makes the character ridiculous, was here a quick pulling up of his trouser leg to show his sock to Olivia; the production emphasized that the real transgression was him wearing a casual suit and confidently taking a seat next to his mistress. His appearance in 2.3 was measured, walking around the edges of the stage as the clowns struggled to fake sobriety. The restraint of his performance was paid off as he read 'Olivia's' letter in 2.5; as he forced it to apply to himself, he sank to his knees, sobbing with gratitude, and cried out, 'I thank my stars! I am happy!' (2.5.165–6). The emotional complexity of this moment allowed for different audience reactions; Donnellan himself suggests that 'in the end our letter scene is often very funny, funny in a horrible way, and upsetting in a funny way' (Sierz 2010: 157). The moment recalled the English-language production of 1986–7, in which Malvolio 'cried joyously, only to be embarrassed that he should be caught doing so in front of an audience (in the theatre)' (Reade 1991: 93). The clowns quietly emerged from behind the upstage drapes, and Toby's quiet delivery of 'Thou hast put him in such a dream, that he must run mad' (2.5.187–8) brought the first half to a sober conclusion. The burden of guilt continued in the second half as Malvolio scornfully threw the straitjacket proffered to him in 3.4 back at his tormentors. A significant transition had Sebastian's ecstatic 'This is the air!' (4.3.1) overlap with Malvolio's 'I am not mad!' (4.2.40) to close 4.2. Malvolio's straitjacketed restraint was placed in pointed contrast with Sebastian's ebullient freedom, the two (would-be) lovers of Olivia polarized in their identities as expressed in their clothes. The production's empathy extended to the very final moment of the play, where the celebrating revellers all took a glass of champagne from the subdued servant. As they prepared to sip, the lights suddenly turned green and the ensemble froze as Malvolio, downstage, leaned towards the audience and spoke, 'I'll be revenged on the whole pack of you' (5.1.371); a triumphant ending for the character on which the production ended. Malvolio's resumption of his steward's garb, and his normal social position, became gleefully central to whatever revenge he was enacting in the drinks.

The resumption of order at the end was also apparent in the unusual decision to have Viola also return to her 'proper' clothes at the production's end. Viola left the stage with Sebastian on Orsino's 'Let me see thee in thy woman's weeds' (5.1.269), and returned in her dress. Whereas the text allows for a homosexual frisson in Orsino's playful refusal to refer to Viola as anything other than Cesario while s/he remains in Cesario's costume, here the production acknowledged that Viola was not a woman *until* re-dressed as one. Yet her reappearance offered a final queering of their relationship, as the character finally presented as a woman to an Orsino who appeared abashed, stepping back from her. He 'saw a stranger, not the thing he fell in love with' (Prescott 2008: 83), and took a moment before stepping back, caressing her face and kissing her. In a production so fluid in its dizzying shifts of gendered identity, the final moment of acknowledgement of an explicit change in gender presentation was given full weight. Orsino's choice to accept Viola in her new/old identity was treated as a choice, with all of the emotional and psychological implications that choice entailed.

The unusual tightness of the Russian ensemble allowed for a *Twelfth Night* that both acknowledged and belied Anne Barton's assertion that 'the little society which they form at the end of the play is far more fragmentary and insubstantial than

the one that had been consolidated in [*As You Like It*]'
(1986: 308). The social construction of identities allowed
for a collective, carnival-esque identity that pushed the play's
serious emotions to unusual prominence, while allowing for
a lightness of touch that found joy even in fear and violence.
The uncanny juxtaposition of emotional reactions made this,
perhaps, one of the play's most potent realizations of the
(literally) upsetting, topsy-turvy atmosphere of carnival.

Female friendship in *As You Like It*

Cheek by Jowl's *As You Like It* was 'the first all-male production
of Shakespeare to gain international popularity ... and to
introduce the convention of the all-male cast to audiences
primed by recent social movements to view as "queer" the
sexual politics of cross-dressing' (Bulman 2008: 80). The
extraordinary success of *As You Like It*, Cheek by Jowl's tenth-
anniversary production and one of only two English-language
Cheek by Jowl productions to be revived with a (mostly)
new cast, saw the production tour over five years to Japan,
Ireland, the UK, the Netherlands, New Zealand, Australia,
Spain, the USA, Brazil, Luxembourg, Russia, Germany, the
Czech Republic, Romania, Bulgaria, Israel and France.[6] Show
reports document the response the production received around
the world, from an audience member encouraging Rosalind to
accept a dukedom to hugely vocal responses to the wrestling
and physical violence (Cheek by Jowl 1991b). In Bulgaria, it
was celebrated as the 'best production that has been seen in the
National Theatre for over ten years' (Cheek by Jowl 1994a).

James Bulman articulates the production's importance thus:
'It gave voice to culturally contested ideas even as they were
being theorized by the academy, leading Alisa Solomon, for
one, to comment on how "a sexist old stage practice" could
unleash an erotic dynamics with the power to deconstruct
gender itself' (2008: 80). Bulman's important article responds

to an overwhelming critical response that argued that the all-male cast rendered gender *unimportant*, accounts 'tantamount to avoidance behaviour … [that] betray a discomfort with the production's sexual politics and a refusal to grapple with the homophobic social attitudes and government policies that … formed the context through which the production should be viewed' (2008: 82). This wasn't true of all reviews; the *Village Voice* review of 6 August 1991, for one, celebrated the production as being 'as gay as a Shakespeare sonnet, its unnameable love bursting gloriously through the seams of a venerated form'. At the same time, the arguments of critics such as Michael Billington that '*As You Like It* is not about sexuality hetero-, homo-, bi-, or trans- but about love' (1991) have some resonance with Donnellan's own recent reflection that the 'chief concern' of both Tony Kushner's *Angels in America* – the play Donnellan and Ormerod worked on at the National immediately before *As You Like It* – and this production 'was the complexity of human love' (Donnellan 2014). Regardless of whether or not the production had a consciously gay agenda, however, the revelatory responses to the production's single-sex conceit speak to the impact of the first modern production to realize the potential of an all-male Shakespeare production; as Shaughnessy notes, 'there was no way, in the climate of its time, that an all-male production of the comedy could not be political' (2017: 181).

John Peter, writing for *The Sunday Times*, was one of several critics to try and articulate a sense of the achievement, and lighted on the words 'feminine' and 'effeminate' in attempting to make his point:

Most Rosalinds, when they are dressed as Ganymede, tend to become irresistibly feminine. Adrian Lester remains a young man playing a girl playing a young man. What dominates his performance is not sensuality but deep feeling. Sensuality is not denied, only held in check. Tom Hollander's Celia is a shrewd, humorous girl, capable of being poisonously demure … [Neither] is ever, for a moment, effeminate, but simply and naturally feminine. It is not a question of merely transcending sexuality or of being in drag, but of actors reaching out towards a different experience and communicating a different mode of being. (1991)

The distinction between 'feminine' and 'effeminate' is here coded as between 'simple and natural' on the one hand and, implicitly, arch and unnatural on the other. That is, the production's achievement was in the 'realness' of the women performed by the male actors, an achievement that seems inherently confused in the critical mind. For Bulman, the effacement of the male body by critics in pursuit of this 'natural' femininity is coded as homophobic, the reviewers comforting themselves by believing in the evoked female body, in order to avoid confronting the implications of two men sharing a love scene. Yet the production repeatedly drew attention to the very absence of that evoked body. Robert Shaughnessy describes one of the key moments:

Rosalind, at the end of her dialogue with Jaques (who, played as a predatory Wildean queen, saw in Ganymede another of the many young men in the forest who caught his wandering fancy), seized his hand and placed it on his/her breast. Performing a gesture that would with a female actor incontrovertibly confirm gender as biological truth, Lester conjured a female body that was pure theatrical fiction. (2017: 189)

Lester's body in this moment performed multiple functions. The male body served both as substrate upon which the performance built *and* the façade that was presented to those onstage. This moment occurred at the start of 4.1, with Orlando present; nonetheless, the shared image of Lester's (real) body and Ganymede's (presented) body convincingly kept Rosalind's gender a secret from him.[7]

Yet the physical, intimate gesture between Jaques and Rosalind, while evoking the 'pure theatrical fiction' of

Rosalind's breast, shared a different truth between those characters, 'a truth of Rosalind's female body that lies beneath the male mask of Ganymede, an essential truth of biology underlying Rosalind's (meta)theatrical representation of herself as a boy' (Mazer 2008: 96), which also stood for an acknowledgement of an emotional aliveness between the two characters. At the moment he touched Rosalind's breast, Jaques was at a moment of crisis. His 'I prithee, pretty youth, let me be better acquainted with thee' (4.1.1–2) was spoken to the departing Silvius rather than to Rosalind, Jaques coming on to the young man, who rejected him while nicking one of his cigarettes. Jaques subsequently sobbed his melancholy into Rosalind's lap, only to pull himself together and resume his usual grousing when Orlando entered; it was in this context that Rosalind shared her secret. The moment served as a gesture of solidarity, even trust, between two unrequited lovers. Jaques's rejection by Silvius produced an empathy in Rosalind that led her to induct Jaques into the secret of her own body, the two characters now collectively responsible for the production of Ganymede/Rosalind's gender. The gesture depended both on the evoked reality of Rosalind's body and the physical reality of Lester's, a 'femininity' that was anything but 'simple'.

Adrian Lester describes something of his experience of the shift in rehearsals from 'playing every woman' to 'playing Rosalind':

During the early rehearsals for *As You Like It* I remember being caught up with the fact that I had to be 'every woman'. I suppose it was fear really. I hadn't grasped any specific elements of character in relation to her sex. I was afraid of looking foolish and was therefore a bit basic and heavy handed in my approach – women do this, women walk like this, women's voices are like this, etc etc. Unfortunately the more I tried to do that, the more stilted and stereotyped my work was becoming. It was during the second week of rehearsals that I had a kind of epiphany, an understanding that has bled into all the characters I have subsequently played. I realised I wasn't playing a woman *per se*, I was playing Rosalind. I went home and had a good long hard look at myself in the mirror. If I was a young woman, I would feel I was too tall, because I was just over six foot. I would feel that my voice was too low, that I was completely flat chested and asexual ... I would feel that I was completely unattractive. As soon as I knew these things to be true for character I started down a path where I could uncover the detail of Rosalind behind the words on the page. (2016)

Lester's comments focus on his own body, acknowledging the features of that body that create cognitive dissonance when reading it as female. Rather than hide the body through prosthetics or layers, he made his body visible – to himself, at least. As Jonathan Holmes puts it, Lester 'began to focus on the social assumptions made about the character in the script, and on those made about himself as a male performer, and to construct his performance in the gap between the two ... Lester's Rosalind was a Rosalind who had suddenly to contend with looking like Adrian Lester' (Holmes 2012: 133). Within Cheek by Jowl's work, this is significant; while costume is essential to a company that travels lightly, Cheek by Jowl's costumes never hide the actor. Lester focuses on how the performance was constructed in relation to Celia:

It's plain to see that in the beginning of the play Celia has all the power. When Rosalind is upset about her father Celia says 'Oh, don't be like that, cheer up,' and Rosalind replies 'What, just cheer up?' Celia goes gets a little annoyed and so Rosalind has to stop thinking of her dad who, for all she knows, could be out in the forest lying dead somewhere, simply because Celia is annoyed. Rosalind has to try and make Celia happy. It's all about this spoiled little rich girl. Once I realised that, and my bookish quotes of fortune, I thought to myself – hold on, she's very quick, quick to the point where she'll hold some of it back in order to make her cousin feel better. And that gave me my Rosalind: incredibly quick witted, bookish, glasses-wearing, collapsed-chested, shrinking in height, not really wanting to look anyone in the eye. I had a thing, a long silk scarf, same colour as my dress tied tightly around my head which pulled my features back, softened my cheekbones and forced me to be aware of my head movement as though I had long hair. I would make her hold onto her book as if it were her safe place. As long as I stayed in my little quiet box I was going to be fine. (2016)

Rosalind and Celia operated as a pair. As with *Twelfth Night*, the company first appeared wearing identical costumes, but as a voice spoke, 'All the world's a stage / And all the men and women merely players' (2.7.140), the actors who would be playing female characters shifted slightly apart from those playing men, emphasizing that gender 'was just one of the many roles we play' (Mazer 2008: 99). The two women emerged together from the ensemble when first mentioned by Charles (1.1.102–7), before walking offstage holding hands. The two established a private space for themselves on a rug centre stage, initially isolated within a closely limited pool of light, and this rug became their private space for the whole of Act 1, to which they returned after Rosalind's banishment (Figure 3). The close relationship between the two women defined the production; as Lester explains, his Rosalind presented herself in relation to what she perceived to be Celia's needs, and thus Lester/Rosalind's transformation throughout the performance reflected the shift in their relationship, as well as the shift in location.

Simon Coates, in the 1994–5 revival, played Celia with distinct overtones of Margaret Thatcher. Celia was privileged and imperious, deeply caring of her friend but arrogant with her father's attendants. When Le Beau (Sean Francis) began laying a rope for the wrestling ring, Celia petulantly kicked it out of shape, resulting in Le Beau being dragged off and having his trousers pulled off by other attendants as punishment. Her overwhelming love for Rosalind manifested as babying. Celia kept Rosalind's head in her lap, stroked her back and hair

FIGURE 3 *Celia (Simon Coates) and Rosalind (Adrian Lester).*
Photograph by John Haynes/Lebrecht Music & Arts.

and spoke in soothing tones. Rosalind tried to take up as little
space as possible by hunching her shoulders and burying her
nose in a book, allowing Celia to dominate.

The fragility of their relationship became clear early on.
Cynthia Marshall notes the pair's 'custom of spitting when
the word "man" was uttered', a custom clearly performed
for Celia's benefit (2004: 91). As Rosalind sighed for 'my
child's father' (1.3.11), however, Celia jumped to her feet
and slapped Rosalind in anger, the latter's interest in a man
a betrayal of their sisterhood. Rosalind raised her own voice
in response, demanding, 'Let me love him for that' (35), the
first time that Lester's deeper range was heard, marking this
as the first time that Rosalind had insisted on Celia hearing
her words. The potential rift between the two, however, was
immediately healed in the confrontation with the Duke (David
Hobbs) that followed. Rosalind delivered her self-defence
while kneeling, and while her voice rose in power and volume,

she broke off suddenly on 'My father was no traitor' (60). The Duke advanced on her, and Celia threw herself in the way, reminding the Duke that Rosalind's presence 'was your pleasure and your own remorse' (67); the Duke slapped her for her trouble and threw her to the floor on 'I cannot live out of her company' (83). The Duke's intolerance of Celia's assertion of independence echoed Celia's own resistance to Rosalind's, and the act of abuse linked father and daughter. Donnellan himself noted that 'Celia ... has an enormous crush on Rosalind' (Hemming 1991), and Bulman insightfully reads into this the 'clear implication ... that the Duke suspected Celia of being infatuated with Rosalind – perhaps of having a sexual relationship with her' (2008: 84), though I am less inclined to read the slap as a homophobic rebuke than as the Duke's reflexive expression of jealousy at his daughter's love for someone who wasn't him. While Celia's defence of Rosalind was a powerful one, it was also reflective of the dynamic that she would spend the subsequent four acts outgrowing.

This dynamic was most evident in the play's second half, in which Celia spent much of her time sitting sullenly at the side or downstage while Rosalind grew into her role as Ganymede. Earlier, when Rosalind had announced she would take on the name 'Ganymede' (1.3.122), she and Celia had giggled together. When Celia announced, with a certain amount of gravitas, that she would be Aliena (125), Rosalind roared, to Celia's distinct displeasure.[8] Celia's good humour was tied to the esteem in which Rosalind held her; as the second half progressed, Rosalind no longer needed Celia's approval. 'Given the affection with which Rosalind and Celia stroked one another in the first act and their custom of spitting when the word "man" was uttered, Rosalind's attachment to Orlando seemed even more of a defection from previous loyalties than usual' (Marshall 2004: 91). As such, 'irritated by the treachery of her friend' (Holland 1992: 128), Celia milked her increasingly rare moments of power, such as knowing who had written the letters hung on Arden's trees (3.2). While Rosalind interrogated her, Celia sat down and wrote in her journal, deliberately ignoring Rosalind. Once Celia confirmed that it was Orlando, she lost her power and Rosalind's attention. Lester ran, grabbed the letters, shrieked and danced about the stage; Celia's annoyance at Rosalind's constant interruptions only increased. The extremity of Rosalind's joy against Celia's increasing aloofness exaggerated the growing separation of the two in the forest, where earlier their differences in temperament had brought them together on Celia's terms.

Such was the mood when Orlando (Scott Handy) finally met Ganymede. As Jaques departed, Orlando reclined on the floor, and Rosalind yanked herself from Celia's restraining hands to speak to him. In breaking away from Celia, Rosalind for the first time made herself completely vulnerable before Orlando, in one of the production's most revelatory decisions. He replied to her 'Do you hear, forester?' (3.2.288–9) with an indifferent 'Very well.' Rosalind faced him and stood there, 'fully expect[ing] to recognise her' (Marshall 2004: 184). The moment lengthened into discomfort and she raised her arms in an awkward shrug, still anticipating his recognition. Thwarted, she pointed at the chain he was wearing, strode across the stage and grabbed it, holding it up to remind him of the gift she had given him; his response, however, was to kick himself away, push her back and ask, 'What would you?' (290) in annoyance. No longer smiling, she stepped back, took off her straw hat to reveal her hair bound in a headscarf and held out her arms in a 'here I am' gesture. Orlando responded by pointing for her to move further away, and then lay back down to resume his writing, leaving Rosalind exposed and devastated.

Where earlier in the production Lester/Ganymede/Rosalind had conjured an imagined breast to create a moment of theatrical solidarity between herself and Jaques, now the character found herself unable to summon up on demand a convincing performance of her own femaleness that Orlando could recognize; the line between Ganymede and Rosalind was so thin that Orlando couldn't see the change. As Donnellan puts it, when Rosalind dresses up as a boy, the thing she most wants in the world is Orlando not to recognize her and think she's somebody else and think she's not a woman, to think she's a man. What she *least* wants is for Orlando not to recognize her and think she's a boy. It's both at the same time – it's not half and half. To be actually not recognized by the person that loves you isn't very nice. (Donnellan 2003: 163)

The image of Rosalind standing, bare-headed, offering herself to Orlando, was thus simultaneously amusing and heartbreaking, read by Rosalind as a rejection of her person rather than her persona.

This rejection allowed for a reading of Rosalind's subsequent actions as a process of training Orlando to 'see' properly. Her distress turned to outrage, expressed in angry deliveries of 'There is no true lover in the forest' (3.2.294) and 'I thank God I am not a woman' (335–6), showing a bitterness hitherto absent from the character. At this point, Carol Rutter suggests, 'she made her decision: she'd *stay* cross-dressed!' (2005: 351). Her anatomization of his lack of love symptoms was genuine, Rosalind angrily accusing him of failing to love. The anger reached him where her open invitation had failed, and Rosalind was taken aback as Orlando accepted Ganymede's offer to teach him; she refused to shake his hand on parting. When Orlando subsequently broke his promise and returned late, therefore, Lester gave full vent to Rosalind's fury. She screamed at his neglect, at which he threw himself onto his knees in a performance of contrition. Rosalind continued her anger into her discussion of horns, 'such as you are fain to be beholding to your wives for' (4.1.54–5), upon which Orlando slapped Rosalind, retorting, 'My Rosalind is virtuous' (57–8). The moment of physical violence (as with *Twelfth Night*, more abrupt than would usually take place in a mixed-gender production) put their relationship at crisis point, with Rosalind screaming directly into Orlando's face, 'I AM YOUR ROSALIND!' (59). Cheek by Jowl's rendering of this all-important line took the text literally, innovatively exploring what is at stake when Rosalind flat-out tells Orlando who she is. The stakes are high and, as always for Cheek by Jowl, 'specific' and 'perfectly paired' (Donnellan 2005: 51): that Orlando will accept me/that he will not accept me.

Celia defused the moment, rescuing and undermining Rosalind with 'He has a Rosalind of a better hue,' a line that caused Orlando to wheel disconcertedly before running into the auditorium, and Rosalind conducted the subsequent 'wooing' with a mixture of playfulness and bitterness. Celia appointed herself the manager of Rosalind's feelings, sitting smugly while Rosalind and Orlando fought, then comforting her when Orlando finally left (prompting another furious outburst from Rosalind on 'Go your ways,' 4.1.170). Celia's jibes about Orlando suggested she was enjoying being proven right, but when Rosalind burst into tears, Celia uncomfortably tried to soothe her by putting hands on her. As soon as Rosalind mentioned Orlando again, however, Celia herself became angry, snatching away a letter Rosalind was holding. As earlier, Celia's sympathy was on her own terms, seeing herself as in competition with Orlando for Rosalind's attentions, and she was scathingly condescending as she tutted, 'Oh coz, coz, coz' (193).

Beautifully, then, the production established a subtle focus on female intimacy, and on the terms on which Rosalind and Celia could maintain the closeness that had been forged under the mutual oppression of Celia's father's court.[9] Freed from this environment and no longer needing one another for protection, the pair's relationship became increasingly resentful as Celia found herself no longer needed. As such, the arrival of Oliver (Jonathan Chesterman) provided resolution. As he began reporting Orlando's encounter with the lion (4.3.97ff), he and Celia sat down together downstage, entirely focused on one another. A sidelined Rosalind tried repeatedly to get attention, Oliver responding to her in annoyance before turning back to Celia; Rosalind's shout of 'What about the bloody napkin?' had the ring of profanity in its frustration. Oliver handed over the napkin and, while he and Celia stared at one another downstage, Rosalind staggered upstage and fainted. Nonetheless, Oliver's arrival balanced the women's relationship and diffused the tension between them.

The production's conclusion drew the two women back together. As 5.4 began, Celia took charge of making the arrangements, lighting candles and bustling about. It was Celia who hurried Rosalind offstage while she was in the middle of triple-checking the conditions to which the other characters had agreed, and the two returned in full wedding dresses downstage while Hymen entered upstage. Rosalind knelt before Orlando. Both Orlando and her father (Hobbs again) stepped towards her in shock; she gently reached out her hand to Orlando, but he stepped back and away three times, finally turning away completely in a move that has been read variously as homophobic fear, disgust, betrayal, disappointment or shock. Rosalind was left standing alone, rejected for the second time in her own person, and this time without ambiguity. She threw her bouquet to the floor and embraced her father, sobbing into his chest. After another pause, Orlando stepped forward and reached out to her, saying, 'If there be truth in sight, you are my Rosalind' (5.4.117). Rosalind initially pulled away, but finally detached from her father and embraced Orlando. They stood looking at one another before kissing, a kiss that went on long and passionately before an embarrassed Celia began a round of applause that brought it to a close.

Yet while this much-discussed ending focused on the resolution of the distorted gender identities and sexual politics between the play's heterosexual lovers, few critics have noted the importance of what followed for resolving the thread of Rosalind and Celia's relationship. Following Orlando and Rosalind's kiss, the Duke revealed Celia as his niece, causing Oliver to kneel to her. Mimicking them, Silvius and Phoebe clicked their fingers at one another to tell the other to kneel before them, before they embraced as equals. But the arrival of Jaques de Boys (Francis again) altered things again, as he brought with him the medal of Duke Frederick. He offered it to Duke Senior, and everyone knelt to him. The Duke then put it around Orlando's neck, christening him his heir, and Rosalind knelt to him. In a reversal of their first meeting, however, Orlando in turn put the medal around her neck; again, everyone knelt. This time, however, Celia was the last to take a knee, giving a prominent eye roll as she did so. This ending was not dark, but completed the reversal of their relationship that had seen Rosalind break out of the subservient, embarrassed, retiring role that had been her lot when isolated with Celia. In discovering her own identity, Rosalind had discovered her own power.

Epilogue

As You Like It, as with *Twelfth Night* before it, used its all-male cast to place emphasis on identity creation and negotiation as central to human interaction. The productions were both hailed as progressive, both in queer terms and (in the case of *As You Like It*) for its integrated cast, Adrian Lester's performance marking the first time a black actor of any gender had taken the role in the UK, and the first time since 1975 'that a male actor of colour was cast in a traditionally white leading role by a national company' (Shaughnessy 2017: 187).[10] In the context of Cheek by Jowl's work, meanwhile, both productions foregrounded the potential of the closely knit ensemble for opening up a play. The work of the collective, producing gender identities within it, allowed the company to explore emotional connections and complexities rarely discovered in productions of either play. Whether Rosalind explicitly telling Orlando who she was or Sir Toby acknowledging his own damage of Maria and Malvolio, the productions epitomized the 'theatrical lying … through [which] we can tell each other the truth' (Reade 1991: 32).

Lester's delivery of *As You Like It*'s epilogue ended the play on a note of celebratory ambiguity. In a winning delivery of what sounded genuinely like an impromptu speech, full of laughter and hesitations, Lester turned on the charm, flirting with the audience and asking them to forgive the play. But then, Lester paused, took off his earrings and whipped off his headscarf, leaving his head lowered for a moment before raising it to stare impassively at the audience. Speaking in his naturally deeper voice 'for the first time in the show' (Shaughnessy 2017: 189), and with short hair, lipstick and necklace all complicating his gender presentation, Lester intoned, 'If I *were* a woman' (Epilogue 16–17); the conditional, perhaps deliberately recalling Touchstone's 'Much virtue in if' (5.4.101), representing for Holmes 'the mutability of identity over time and space' (2012: 134). The sudden seriousness of the final lines, delivered with the subtlest of smiles but a hint of sadness, drew attention to the conditionality of the performed body – and the possibilities and limitations inherent in gendered identity. Lester's 'if', finally, came back to the stakes at the heart of Cheek by Jowl's practice, with 'If I were' shadowed by the unspoken opposite: 'If I were *not*.' 'The invocation of the theatrical,' Mazer argues, 'both foregrounds the performativity of gender and erases it … the biological markers of the actor's gender identity are both essential and inescapable and at the same time invisible and occasionally irrelevant' (2008: 100–1). For Rosalind (as for Celia, Maria, Viola, Olivia and the rest), whether their gendered identity was constructed by the men who saw them or whether it was claimed by themselves, the blurring of gender boundaries celebrated and questioned the performative possibilities of playing with 'if'.

4

Cutting and cross-cutting: filmic space and the text

Cymbeline (2007) and *The Tempest* (2011–)

In the previous three chapters, I have referred repeatedly to some of Cheek by Jowl's core stylistic conceits, which have characterized the company's output since the early 1980s – the appearance of characters as they are spoken about and the overlapping scene transition – and in this chapter, I pause to unpack these concepts in more detail. Despite the ubiquity of these features of Cheek by Jowl's productions, they are surprisingly under-discussed. Maria Shevtsova offers some important insight in her discussion of Donnellan's production of *Le Cid* for the Avignon Festival in 1998–9:

> Corneille's heroics … are cut down to size through such devices as the ghost figure (not in Corneille) of Chimène's father, whom Rodrigue, the protagonist and Chimène's lover, kills to avenge the death of his own father. This 'ghost' stalks the lovers more like a voyeur than a disapproving

father fixated on the rules of duty. ... His gaze is upon Chimène, which illustrates Donnellan's notion of 'target' – *she* is the actor's target rather than his character's internal feelings. (2005: 234)

Shevtsova's alignment of offstage characters with Donnellan's 'target' draws on the principle of externalization that Donnellan has used in the past to help actors overcome 'blocks' that emerge when actors become 'obsessed about their internal state to the point that they are scanning themselves internally to make sure they are showing the right thing' (Donnellan 2018). The target 'always exists outside and at a measurable distance' and 'exists before you need it' (Donnellan 2005: 20). The target, though, as I explained in Chapter 1, is a tool for actors rather than something that can be seen by audiences. The visible figures who intrude on the world of a scene instead testify to the company's unique understanding of space.

The appearance of offstage characters populating the world of Cheek by Jowl's productions makes for a fluid slippage of space that also insists on the implications of the action on all characters. As Paul Prescott puts it, referring to *Othello* (2004), 'the central quintet (the two couples and Cassio) rarely left our sight, their presences serving not only to illustrate and enrich the action but also to remind the audience of the touching impotence of the slandered' (2008: 78). In a particular moment, discussed also by Christopher Innes and Maria Shevtsova, Cassio and Desdemona sat 'frozen with their backs to the audience as Iago lies to Othello about her (false) sexual encounter with Cassio' (2013: 215); as Iago's description became graphic, 'Cassio mimed placing his leg over Iago's thigh [and] across the stage Desdemona groaned, her back arching in sexual desire' (Prescott 2008: 78). The use of the frozen (and not-so-frozen) figures allowed the scene to slip seamlessly between real and imagined space, eliding the distinction between Iago's words and the image in Othello's mind's eye.

Innes and Shevtsova refer to this device as a 'tableau-freeze … signifying that [characters] belong to the whole story of the play' (2013: 215). On Cheek by Jowl's stage, actors interact within a fluid spatial environment that shifts according to the scene's interpretive demands, and keeps in full view the larger narrative and emotional stakes of the scene and play. The 'tableau-freeze' is just one of the tools in Cheek by Jowl's dramaturgical toolbox, and it is worth noting that this elides not just space but *time*. It occurs in two major contexts:

Asides: when a character delivers an aside, others on stage usually freeze. While this is not unique to Cheek by Jowl, the company uses the device to foreground the bodies of the frozen actors as the subject of discussion, positioning the soliloquiser in relation to that which has prompted their thought. I call this the *frozen subject*.

Talking about offstage characters: in this usage, characters spoken about are brought on from offstage or forward from the ensemble. In these instances, the characters are often not still but moving, sometimes speaking. This gives the primary speaker a moving, living focus, making their mental visualization collectively visible. It often also has a useful storytelling function, introducing figures who have not yet appeared. I call this the *projected subject*.

Both frozen and projected subjects render the implications of the present action visible to audiences. The temporal and spatial connection associates the spoken word with an image that is not diegetically present, but creates an emotional attachment that transcends the scene's *locus*. It opens up fresh interpretive possibilities as the actor plays against a visualization of what their character is imagining: Cary Mazer observes of a moment in *Cymbeline* (2007) that 'while Tom Hiddleston's Posthumus cursed Imogen in 2.5, she materialized on stage and his hands moved slowly over her body without touching her, revealing his simultaneous desire and disgust' (Wayne 2017: 121).

While the eschewal of realistic space is an obviously theatrical technique, the blurring of narrative space – particularly the juxtaposition of spoken words and visual images that relate to each other thematically but not temporally or spatially – is a convention of film. As David Bordwell and Kristin Thompson put it,

> Sound has a spatial dimension because it comes from a *source*. Our beliefs about that source have a powerful effect on how we understand the sound ... Viewers understand that certain sounds seem to come from the story world, while others come from outside the space of the story events. We've learned these conventions so thoroughly that we usually don't have to think about which type of sound we're hearing at any moment. At many times, though, a film's narration deliberately blurs boundaries between different spatial categories. A play with the conventions can be used to puzzle or surprise the audience, to create humor or ambiguity, or to suggest thematic implications. (2015: 284)

One of the most obvious examples of this in film is the narrative voice-over, in which the narrator by and large does not exist within the depicted world, but comments on it from an ambiguous space between the viewer and the image. The words change the image; the image focuses the meaning of the words. In Cheek by Jowl's use of frozen and projected subjects, the same logic is used to mould the text and construct characters, creating arcs for individuals that extend beyond their own lines. Significantly for Cheek by Jowl's work, the narrative voice-over is also a privilege afforded to characters as an editing function, when the sound of the previous scene continues over a visual cutaway in order to make a connection between the two – a voice that says, 'I wonder where she is now,' while the screen depicts the person being talked about. This editing technique is so pervasive in Cheek by Jowl's theatre work that critics regularly refer to these productions using filmic language: Julia Rank comments on 'Donnellan's cinematic style that slices from one scene to another' (2012); Mazer refers to scenes as 'cross-cut' (Wayne 2017: 121); and Charles Isherwood discusses the 'fluid, almost cinematic, speed recalling the sharp cutting of a Hitchcock movie' (2007). As Donnellan himself says, 'we love film … we would have done a lot of film if films didn't take so long to set up! And, of course, if we could have retained our independence' (Donnellan 2018).

The cutting is most apparent as an editing technique in the overlapping transitions between scenes, or what Paul Prescott calls 'headlining' (2008: 78), which I consider to be the company's signature technique (see Figure 1). Cheek by Jowl's work eschews scene changes and never interrupts the momentum of a dramatic arc. Instead, the company's innovative practices of cutting and rearranging create scenes that overlap. As Prescott succinctly describes it,

> After the penultimate line of scene A, the first line of scene B is pitched across the playing space. The last line of scene A then prompts whatever scene change needs to take place – a lighting shift, a relocated chair, a reconfiguration of bodies – with no loss of tension before scene B continues … to produce a sense of simultaneity and unceasing momentum. (2008: 78)

As the words of scenes are heard over the image of newly arrived characters, Cheek by Jowl connects dramatic and interpretive tissue, and extends its use of frozen and projected subjects into the transitions. This technique compresses time and elides spatial boundaries in a theatrical equivalent to the dissolve of film editing, insisting on the connectedness of the play; Judith Greenwood, the company's longest-serving lighting designer, refers to these moments as '"meanwhile" states [in which] on a film you would be going between two locations; the only difference is we have them both on stage at the same time' (2016). Further, careful cutting of the text allows the opening lines of the new scene to comment on the action that has just concluded. When Jodie McNee's Imogen, at the start of *Cymbeline* 1.6, spoke 'A father cruel, and a step-dame false' while Gwendoline Christie's Queen was still frozen in the process of her exit from 1.5, the company extended and focused its judgement of the Queen, reinforcing a visual connection between the two characters and physicalizing Imogen's fears.

In this chapter, my two case studies illustrate Cheek by Jowl's work with cutting – both of the text and of the editing process that marks transitions. First, I consider the promptbook of *Cymbeline*, a production that underwent an unusually innovative process of dramaturgical crafting in order to clarify the narrative and emotional stakes. I then move on to the company's second production of *The Tempest*, premiered by the Russian company in 2011, whose visualization of offstage and projected characters particularly emphasized the visual qualities of the play and the processes of dramatic recreation.

Cutting *Cymbeline*

Cymbeline is a play that presents 'notoriously difficult' staging issues (Wojciehowski 2015: xx), as well as being one of the longest in the canon. Donnellan himself notes it has a 'problematic structure … although that may be part of its mysterious grandeur' (Donnellan 2009: 82). Cheek by Jowl's celebrated 2007 production thus offers an ideal case study for exploring the ways in which the company adjusts the text throughout rehearsal in order to get to the heart of the play. It also gives the lie to Simon Reade's claim that 'very little is snipped away, so the plays really do speak for themselves, run at a full though not a fulsome length, and never iron out the apparent inconsistencies but confront them head-on' (1991: 68). Considering Cheek by Jowl's reputation for 'care for the text as a discrete verbal composition requiring pristine exposition, enunciation and diction' (Shevtsova 2005: 233), it can be surprising – though not contradictory – to realize how much of that text is pruned. The promptbook for Cheek by Jowl's version of *Cymbeline* contains approximately 1,676 lines, or 51 per cent of the Folio text's 3,258 lines.[1] On a scene by scene basis, this breaks down as in Table 1.

Table 1 *Scene-by-scene comparison of line length of Cheek by Jowl's* Cymbeline *and the Arden text*

Scene	Arden text	Cheek by Jowl text	Percentage retained
1.1	180 lines	142 lines	79
1.2	39 lines	17 lines	44
1.3	40 lines	27 lines	68
1.4	175 lines	102 lines	58
1.5	87 lines	50 lines	57
1.6	209 lines	144 lines	69
2.1	64 lines	16 lines	25
2.2	51 lines	38 lines	75
2.3	156 lines	92 lines	59
2.4	152 lines	123 lines	81
2.5	34 lines	23 lines	68
3.1	85 lines	54 lines	64
3.2	82 lines	46 lines	56
3.3	107 lines	63 lines	59
3.4	193 lines	82 lines	42
3.5	163 lines	79 lines	48
3.6	93 lines	58 lines	62
3.7	16 lines	0 lines	0
4.1	25 lines	13 lines	52
4.2	401 lines	185 lines	46
4.3	46 lines	13 lines	28

Scene	Arden text	Cheek by Jowl text	Percentage retained
4.4	54 lines	26 lines	48
5.1	33 lines	30 lines	91
5.2	18 lines	15 lines	83
5.3	94 lines	27 lines	29
5.4	177 lines	34 lines	19
5.5	484 lines	177 lines	37

Perhaps the most important thing that emerges from Table 1 is the pervasiveness of Cheek by Jowl's strategies of adaptation. Whereas in some productions entire subplots might be cut, here the strategy was to streamline throughout.[2] Only one scene (3.7) is completely missing, a scene cut in most productions for its relative redundancy. On the other hand, no scene retains all its language; even 5.1, which is 91 per cent of its Folio length, only reaches this figure through the introduction of new dialogue between Posthumus and Iachimo (represented in dumbshow in the Folio). Far from Charles Isherwood's assertion that '"Cymbeline," whether it is called a romance or a tragicomedy or a whatnot, is about as undistillable as Shakespeare plays get' (2007), Cheek by Jowl's cut proves that the play is eminently distillable.

Cymbeline begins in the Folio with a seventy-line conversation between two anonymous gentlemen who introduce the main characters. In Cheek by Jowl's version, the sequence runs to nineteen lines, attributed in the promptbook to actors rather than characters.[3]

> LAURENCE [Caius]
>   I pray you tell me sir, what is the cause of this disquiet?
> DAVID [ensemble]
>   Imogen, the King's daughter, the heir of all his kingdom,
>   ~~Cymbeline has~~ *He hath* purposed unto his wife's sole son.
>   But quite athwart her father's high command

The Princess ~~Imogen~~ refers herself
Unto a poor but worthy gentleman ~~of the court~~, one
Posthumus Leonatus.
Alack good *gentle* man, and therefore banished Britain
by the King.
MARK [ensemble]
   Is she his only child?
DAVID [ensemble]
   The only child of Royal Cymbeline.
DAN [Arviragus]
   He had two sons, *brothers to this royal Imogen.*
JOHN [Guiderius]
   The eldest of them at three years old,
DAN [Arviragus]
   I'the swathing-clothes the other, from their nursery
   Were stol'n, and to this hour no guess in knowledge
   Which way the brother princes were ta'en.
   Nor know what was their fate.
RYAN [Belarius]
   When, sir, did this happen?
~~JOHN~~/DAN
   Some twenty years ago.
RYAN [Belarius]
   That a king's children ~~could~~ *should* be so strangely stolen.
LOLA [Helen]
   Here comes the ~~new~~ queen, a widow that ~~Royal
   Cymbeline~~ *the King* hath married but of late. (Cheek by
   Jowl 2007b: 2)

Much of this text is adapted from the original, but compressed.
To look at it another way, this section of 1.1 has nineteen turns
in the Folio text. The above is made up of a rewrite of turns two
and three, a transferred line from turn seven and rewrites of
turns twelve to sixteen and nineteen. The compression focuses
attention on key characters and their immediate relationships
to one another, and the distribution of the lines around a series
of simple visual tableaux infused them with visual meaning.

To the sound of thunder, drapes rose and revealed the company grouped around the stage – some standing, some sitting. An older man (David Collings), wearing a suit, was sat in a chair at the centre; a young woman (Jodie McNee) in a red dress was sat on the floor near him. As a recorded waltz played, Collings stood, walked over to McNee and raised her to her feet, the other figures watching them. McNee pulled away and walked to the side of the stage, and Collings clicked his fingers to stop the music. At this point, the ensemble began speaking. As the second speaker said 'Imogen,' McNee turned to Collings, identifying the figures as Imogen and Cymbeline. After 'sole son' (meaning Cloten), all the figures onstage began moving. Imogen took the hand of a young man (Tom Hiddleston) and brought him before Cymbeline, just as the speaker said, 'Posthumus Leonatus'; even at this early stage, the production identified Hiddleston's body with the two characters he would be playing. Cymbeline angrily separated the lovers and, as 'banished Britain' was spoken, Posthumus began walking away backwards, his eyes remaining on Imogen and his hand outstretched.

On 'only child', Imogen also began moving away, coming closer to her father as she watched Posthumus recede. At this point, the narrators entered the frame. Daniel Percival and John MacMillan took over the narration as it reached the story of their characters, Arviragus and Guiderius. They walked towards Cymbeline as they spoke of their kidnapping, forming a family portrait, with Guiderius to the side of Cymbeline, Cymbeline's hand on Arviragus's shoulder and Imogen sitting before them. From upstage, Ryan Ellsworth's voice boomed out, interrupting the younger men. On 'strangely stolen', Guiderius and Arviragus left the family portrait and walked towards the man who would foster them. Imogen and Cymbeline were left facing a finely dressed young woman (Gwendoline Christie) who had been sitting onstage throughout and who a female member of the Chorus now introduced as the Queen, launching straight into 1.2.

The efficiency of the introductions in this sequence is typical of Cheek by Jowl's narrative clarity, but this clarity is remarkably complex. Initially, the production began with a series of *projected* subjects as the anonymous voices brought the central figures to life in dumbshow. As Guiderius and Arviragus took over the commentary, however, and interacted with the figures they were talking about, there was a spatiotemporal shift that turned Imogen and Cymbeline into *frozen* subjects who were physicalizations of the brothers' understanding and articulation of their own narrative. Percival/Arviragus and MacMillan/Guiderius elided the distinction between Chorus and characters, logically incompatible with the play world but establishing the backstory that is still alive for the characters: 'You look at the story of the play, say *Cymbeline*, and ask, What would it really be like if two children got kidnapped – what would that actually be like? What would it really be like to find them again?' (Sierz 2010: 157). The dramaturgy connected the lines to the bodies with which they would be most importantly associated, and the emergence of the family portrait from the Chorus implanted an image that drove the sense of emotional loss throughout the production.

Cheek by Jowl rarely tell without showing, turning exposition into dramatic dialogue, as in their rendition of 5.3.1–51, Posthumus's report of the battle, which in the promptbook survives as a fifteen-line section attributed to 'Chorus'.[4] In performance, the lines were spoken by named characters, who I insert in square brackets.

[CHORUS] All was lost. [CYMBELINE] The king taken
    Of his wings destitute, the army broken,
[SOLDIERS] And but the backs of Britons seen, all flying
    Through a straight lane, ditched and walled with turf
    The enemy full-hearted, lolling the tongue with slaught'ring
[BELARIUS] All at once, a peasant soldier athwart the lane
[GUIDERIUS] He with two striplings-lads more like to till
    A pelting farm [ARVIRAGUS] than to commit such
        slaughter,
[BELARIUS, GUIDERIUS, ARVIRAGUS] Stand, stand.
    [GUIDERIUS] These three, – 'gan to look
    And to grin like lions. [ARVIRAGUS] Then began
    A rout of the Roman enemy. [GUIDERIUS] Heavens,
        how they wound!

[ARVIRAGUS] Some slain before, some dying.
[GUIDERIUS] Are now each one the slaughterman of twenty.
[CYMBELINE] There was a fourth, an unknown British soldier
    Made the affront with them. (Cheek by Jowl 2007b: 84)

Posthumus's report became, in this efficient sequence, spatially and temporally compressed into the mouths of the characters who performed the actions, they speaking in the third person while performing physical representations of those acts. The sequence superbly expanded Guiderius and Arviragus's roles, having the two complete one another's sentences in a show of unity while directly depicting their courage in battle. 'Stand, stand' – reported speech in the original – became a moment of first-person action, the three grouped together and defending Cymbeline. The spatiotemporal slippage was extended in the completion of the sequence by the early adoption of the Second Captain's lines 'There was a fourth man, in a silly habit / That gave th'affront with them' (86–7). Although the lines are about Posthumus, they were spoken by Cymbeline to anticipate the King's forgiveness of the younger man. Running downstage, Posthumus revealed himself and announced,

'Twas I, Posthumus, in mine own woe charm'd,
Could not find death where I did hear him groan,
Nor feel him where he was struck.

The 'preposterous' chronology, borrowing Pascale Aebischer's appropriation of the term as spatial and temporal inversion, a 'disruption of hierarchy and the "natural" order of things' (2013: 84), uncoupled the linear events of the battle from Posthumus's belated account *until* this point, when Posthumus emerged as a character and segued into his real-time rejection of his costume and subsequent arrest. The effect was uniquely theatrical and filmic, using montage and voice-over to reorganize the events in chronological order, but with an extreme compression of space–time that sketched the events with an eye to dramatic clarity and character progression.

The compression is also noticeable in the case of long speeches. For example, Iachimo's explanation of his plot and actions in the final scene takes up sixty-seven lines in the Arden edition, but only ten in the Cheek by Jowl promptbook. I underline the borrowings in the below:

Arden

Your daughter's chastity: there it begins.
He spake of her as Dian had hot dreams
And she alone were cold, whereat I, wretch,
Made scruple of his praise; and wagered with him
Pieces of gold 'gainst this which then he wore
Upon his honoured finger, to attain
In suit the place of's bed and win this ring
By hers and mine adultery. He, true knight,
No lesser of her honour confident
Than I did truly find her, stakes this ring,
And would so had it been a carbuncle
Of Phoebus' wheel, and might so safely had it
Been all the worth of's car. Away to Britain
Post I in this design. Well may you, sir,
Remember me at court, where I was taught
Of your chaste daughter the wide difference
'Twixt amorous and villanous. Being thus quenched
Of hope, not longing, mine Italian brain
'Gan in your duller Britain operate
Most vilely; for my vantage, excellent.
And to be brief, my practice so prevailed,
That I returned with simular proof enough
To make the noble Leonatus mad
By wounding his belief in her renown
With tokens thus, and thus: averring notes
Of chamber-hanging, pictures, this her bracelet –
O cunning, how I got it – nay some marks
Of secret on her person, that he could not
But think her bond of chastity quite cracked,

> I having ta'en the forfeit. Whereupon –
> <u>Methinks I see him now</u> – (5.5.179–209)

Promptbook

> Your daughter's chastity. There it begins
> I wager'd to win this ring of him
> But your chaste daughter taught to me
> the difference 'Twixt love and villainy.
> So I did feign a show ^{with} seeming proof enough
> To make the noble Posthumus run mad,
> Methinks, I see him now. (Cheek by Jowl 2007b: 92)

There are several features worthy of note here. Firstly, the first and last lines of the speech are preserved, a feature that interestingly recalls Simon Palfrey and Tiffany Stern's note on the importance of cue lines, often preserved even when the content of a speech is revised, as in different texts of *Hamlet* (2007: 8). Secondly, the promptbook version clarifies throughout. Leonatus consistently becomes Posthumus; 'simular proof' becomes 'seeming proof'; and the central clause changes from passive to active, giving Imogen the agency and streamlining syntax. Thirdly, there is a general adherence to metre, including adding 'run' to the penultimate line to compensate for the loss of a syllable in turning 'Leonatus' into 'Posthumus'. While the number of feet varies between four and six, the rhythm remains roughly iambic. But the most fascinating change comes in the reconstruction of lines from scattered words, the sentence from 180–6 converted into a single short line that strips out imagery and boils it down to the key action: 'I wager'd to win this ring of him' ('wager'd' was trisyllabic in performance). The new line privileges the visual symbol of the ring, retaining the minimum necessary information to recall earlier events to the audience's mind.

Cheek by Jowl cuts to what the company considers to be most important in the play. Throughout *Cymbeline*, this meant privileging the family and other interpersonal relationships that drove the production's sense of loss and need for reconnection. While Peter J. Smith notes that 'The dynastic struggles of Cymbeline's dysfunctional family, the one-upmanship of Posthumus and Iachimo and the political loggerheads of England and Italy were tiny episodes within a huge empty space' (2007: 352), this empty space (as with *Macbeth* and *The Duchess of Malfi*) placed more emphasis on the human subjects speaking. *Cymbeline*, as Valerie Wayne argues, is a 'recapitulatory play' (2017: 28), both in its evocation of elements from Shakespeare's previous work and in the sheer volume of stories told during its running time. By juxtaposing these stories with the bodies of the relevant characters, Donnellan and Ormerod used montage to define the emotional arcs at the play's heart.

The effect of montage was most obvious in the decision to cast Tom Hiddleston as both Cloten and Posthumus. Hiddleston's much-remarked dual performance created a world in which 'Posthumus and Cloten are, physically at least, interchangeable; the irrationality of desire is all that separates them' (Smith 2007: 353). Katherine Goodland takes this further:

As he morphed back and forth before our eyes between Cloten and Posthumous [*sic*], alternately removing and donning his spectacles, Tom Hiddleston revealed that the two characters are really one. Posthumous sans spectacles is Cloten, his inner blindness to Imogen's virtue, manifested in his external myopia, allows Iachimo to lead him further into human darkness when he arranges for her murder. And, as this production indicates, Iachimo's capacity for malice, especially with respect to women, is also an aspect of Posthumous's nature. Shakespeare often works in triangles of characters (Hamlet, Fortinbras, Laertes; Desdemona, Emilia, Bianca) in ways that help to illuminate important similarities and differences in their natures. Posthumous's nature, however virtuous, also contains aspects of Cloten and Iachimo. This production

> reveled in these patterns of three, deploying blocking in which there were frequently triangles of characters or triangles created by light and shadow on the stage. (2007: 138)

Hiddleston's onstage transformations between the two men inevitably drew attention to the similarities as well as differences between Cloten and Posthumus, and the fluidity with which characters could appear extra-diegetically blurred the lines between them even further. When Cloten donned Posthumus's trench-coat in order to disguise himself, it was impossible to distinguish between an actor changing between characters and a character disguising himself as another; Posthumus's misogyny and Cloten's cruelty were identically embodied, and Imogen's reactions to the two men aligned. Cloten's repeated harping on Imogen's valuing of him less than Posthumus's 'meanest garment' further drew attention to the fluid boundaries between the two characters, that 'meanest garment' both the discriminating identifier and the object that allowed them to become one in Cloten's final moments and in Imogen's heartbreaking 'recognition' of the headless corpse. To James Shapiro, the doubling suggested the 'uncertain and threatened masculinity [that] is the central problem of comedies' (2016). For Donnellan, 'the most important thing is Posthumus's continual, substantial material presence, although in another guise', his embodied presence making him a persistent focus for Imogen (Donnellan 2009: 78).

Finally, the spatial and temporal collapses came to their most pathos-laden conclusion in 3.2, in a deeply ironic sequence that might be considered a three-dimensional rendition of split screen. Posthumus and his projected image of Imogen remained onstage from the end of 2.5 while Pisanio (Richard Cant) soliloquized about the letter he had received. As she was cued, the projected Imogen became the real Imogen, taking the letter from Pisanio as Posthumus moved around in front of her. He walked slowly upstage as she spoke about him:

O, learn'd indeed were that astronomer
That knew the stars as I his characters;
He'ld lay the future open.

The irony of Imogen knowing Posthumus's 'characters' but not his 'character' was underscored through Posthumus's haunting presence, his slow and deliberate movements contrasting with her happy dance as she read his letter. Although Imogen was talking about Posthumus, she was denied the usual privilege of a projected subject; Hiddleston continued to embody the real, murderously minded Posthumus, rendering her obliviousness to his deceit all the more upsetting. In moments such as these, Cheek by Jowl's manipulation of theatrical space through cutting and cross-cutting, projected and frozen subjects, created a revolutionary structural coherence rooted in the connections, known and unknown, between characters.

Weathering *The Tempest*

The Tempest, which premiered in France in January 2011, was the fourth collaboration between Cheek by Jowl and the Chekhov International Theatre Festival, and the second Shakespeare. By this time, Donnellan had been working with many of the same actors for a decade, and the closeness of the ensemble was evident; 'astonishingly they became an ensemble just like that, and, suddenly it was as if we had been together forever' (Donnellan 2009: 80–1). *The Tempest* marked an important stylistic innovation for the company. Whereas Cheek by Jowl's productions of the first decade of the twenty-first century had mostly taken place on a bare stage – from the traverse stagings of *Othello* (2004) and *Troilus and Cressida* (2008) to the deep, black spaces of *Cymbeline* (2007) and *Three Sisters* (2005–) – *The Tempest* ushered in the 2010s with a wall featuring doors, a simple piece of set that would recur in *'Tis Pity She's a Whore*

(2011–14) and *Ubu Roi* (2013–15) (see Chapter 5) and later *Périclès* (2018). This wall allowed for projection, the opening storm breaking in video across the wall, adding a new element of filmic language to the company's palette.[5]

The company's rehearsals included a period 'in the woods' (Donnellan and Ormerod 2016), a pre-rehearsal development period that also functions as an extended ensemble-building endeavour. As Anna Khalilulina puts it, 'it's a place where a group of people becomes united, moulds into a team. We start speaking the same language, everyone is equal, everyone works equally hard' (2017). The gap of time between the 'woods' and the main rehearsal period also allows for more extensive scenic development, allowing for instance for construction of this production's set. For *The Tempest*, a particularly influential *étude* shaped some of the approaches to the finished production.

ORMEROD: The water in *The Tempest*: we rehearsed that on an island, on a beach, with a lake … every aspect of *The Tempest* is imbued with water, and the sea, and the shipwreck, and they improvised the shipwreck. They actually did that on water.

DONNELLAN: They, for us, performed this extraordinary *étude*. I gave them a long talk about 'we split, we split', so it's like the dualistic splitting – it's not 'we sink, we sink', it's 'we split', this thing going into two, that's going to be put back into one at the end of the play. And they said, 'Okay, we'll do that!' and told us to go off and have coffee or something to eat, and then got us to come down to the lake and describe what we saw. They lashed two boats together, took it into the middle of the lake, and then the two boats separated and sank, and then they all started to drown, and started to come out of the lake. It took about twenty minutes to do, covered in mud, and it was just amazing, an amazing moment. And we just used it. (Donnellan and Ormerod 2016)

The *étude* informed the eventual production in several ways. At a literal level, this was an especially *wet* production of *The Tempest*. Ariel (Andrei Kuzichev) followed the beached nobles around as they acclimatized to the island, pouring water from a watering can that became their lifeline. Later, in an extended bit of hilarious comic business, the same watering can followed Trinculo (Ilya Ilyin) around no matter how many times he changed position to get out of its way.[6] In scenes reminiscent of the famous *Morecambe and Wise* skit on *Singin' in the Rain*, Trinculo's attempts to flee through doors only resulted in whole buckets of water being thrown in his face and an eventual resignation to his damp fate.

But more importantly, the company's use of projected and frozen subjects served to emphasize the same separation that had characterized *Cymbeline* and was discovered in the above *étude* for this production. The opening scene placed Prospero (Igor Yasulovich) downstage, sitting on a crate. Upstage, the three doors in the blank wall began to bang softly as if in wind, and a projection of stormy skies filled the wall. The two side doors then flew open and mariners, nobles and waiters (desperately balancing champagne flutes) appeared in the openings. As the mariners screamed and hauled at ropes, the nobles shouted abuse. Amidst this, Miranda (Anna Khalilulina), 'a Raphael angel of a girl with the habits of a feral cat' (Rutter 2012: 465), emerged from the central door, running forward and throwing herself onto the floor next to her father, sobbing in terror.

The simple opening juxtaposed the concurrently occurring events, cause and effect, while foregrounding Prospero's agency in creating the storm from silence. Prospero's prior presence, not an unusual feature of productions of *The Tempest*, cast the nobles and mariners as his projected subjects, their presence onstage providing an embodied visualization of his action – only this time, the projected subjects actually experienced the effects. Prospero continued to produce subjects throughout 1.2. On mention of their names (66, 121), Antonio (Evgeny Samarin) and Alonso (Mikhail Zhigalov) emerged from the doors. Antonio sat downstage with a ledger, which he handed to Alonso as he entered, while Prospero and Miranda crouched at the edges of the stage, Miranda looking at them in fear and fascination. Prospero's use of the subjects for Miranda's benefit cast him as a director, eliding Prospero's magic with Cheek by Jowl's usual practice. Fascinatingly, the two men's presence ended with the coup; on 'did Antonio open the gates of Milan' (129–30), Antonio and Alonso looked at one another, opened the upstage doors and left, their visual presence ending at exactly the moment when, in his narrative, Prospero lost control.[7] This variation on the projected subject strengthened the importance of affect, evoking the embodied presence of the object of the character's attention during a time of intense emotional reflection, and then vanishing it at a point of trauma.

Informed by the experience of dragging themselves through the mud, this was an unusually unsentimental *Tempest* in which the characters experienced labour and trauma. Prospero was a shirt-and-braces-wearing patriarch, angry and prone to outbursts, and brusque with Miranda. Miranda, meanwhile, in one of the most important redefinitions of the character in recent times, betrayed an upbringing devoid of social niceties or etiquette. Khalilulina was encouraged to see her 'not as a princess or a lyric heroine', but as something wilder: 'the other actors showed me wolves and jerboas' (2017). As Prospero broke down describing his people's love for him (1.2.141), Miranda tried to comfort him, eventually wrapping her leg around his chest from behind while rubbing his arms and shoulders. Their relationship was physical and instinctive; Prospero frequently clipped her around the head, and she responded with a combination of fear, defiance and awe. Their household was completed by Caliban (Alexander Feklistov), a presence so familiar that Miranda thought nothing of taking her top off in front of him as she prepared her bath. Half-naked, she laughed at her reflection in a golden bowl, and Caliban looked and laughed with her; this moment of apparent innocence was interrupted by a furious Prospero who dashed over, hit Miranda and shoved her shift back into her hands while shooing Caliban away. Feklistov describes the relationship thus:

His conflict with Prospero gives his life a purpose, revenge feeds him as charcoals feed the oven. And yet he willingly submits to Prospero and he even feels love for the family. His attitude towards Miranda is very special. Declan's fantasy was that they grew up together. We did *études* when they teach little Caliban etiquette at the table. But my Mowgli sadly was not able to learn those lessons. (2016)

The three operated as dysfunctional family, the two men working together to fill buckets for Miranda's wash so that Prospero could scrub her legs and neck; and when Prospero took off his belt to thrash Caliban for referring to the attempted rape, Miranda took Caliban's side, clutching at her father's arm to prevent violence against the servant.

The split of the *étude* was thus realized metaphorically in the emotional distance that separated characters, a brusque care that spilled easily into physical violence and that made physical intimacy less than entirely secure; it was realized also in the relationship between Alonso and Pavel Kuzmin's Sebastian, the latter of whom stroked his brother's head gently even while plotting to murder him. Ferdinand (Yan Ilves) and Miranda were also simultaneously close and separate. Ferdinand first appeared suspended upside down behind a door, as one of Prospero's projected subjects, before being disgorged onto land. Miranda's animalistic impulses took over as she crawled towards and prodded him before throwing a bucket of water in his face to wake him up. Ferdinand, on waking, mimicked her, crawling towards her. The fascinated Miranda slapped him experimentally; an aroused Ferdinand pulled her towards him, but she bit him on the leg. They faced one another, she snarling and smiling, he wary, before he pounced, pushed her onto her back and spread her legs. The sight of Ferdinand forcing himself on Miranda while she roared with oblivious laughter offered a disconcerting image of the individuals' entirely different understanding of what was happening. While David Lindley has complained about productions that treat Ferdinand as a potential rapist (2013:

90), this was only part of what was happening here. Miranda and Ferdinand were both attracted to one another, but she was only acting on impulse while he was in full awareness, and any relationship entered into on such unequal terms cannot but be abusive. Prospero struggled to separate the two, and when Prospero finally put a rope around Ferdinand's neck and dragged him out, Miranda let out a howl.

The split was most literally realized, however, in the casting of five Ariels. While Kuzichev, in black shirt and trousers, played the primary figure, four identically dressed actors shared the embodiment of the character's disparate, island-spanning presence. Often, Kuzichev's Ariel stood atop the wall, watching as one of his avatars poured water on the nobles' heads; at other times, he led them as a troupe of musicians. The splitting of his physical manifestation made the character at times intimidating – at his first summoning, the doors flew open to reveal three black-clad figures standing behind them, before Kuzichev entered. Ariel's implicit power prompted defensive hostility from Prospero, who tortured the spirit with the memory of Sycorax; Ariel writhed on the floor and held out his arms, pleading with him to stop in an evocation of Miranda's pleas for Caliban and Ferdinand (all contributing to the sense of Prospero's harshness). While Ariel's multiple selves were often comic, they also suggested something of the character's fragmentation.

The production thus set up a number of divisions – physical, emotional, of understanding and empathy, of self – that would be resolved by the production's end, and Cheek by Jowl's scene transitions emphasized these points by thematically juxtaposing the different groups on the island. An early beautiful example aligned Caliban and Ferdinand. As Ariel appeared to sing 'Full fathom five' (1.2.396), a chastened Caliban (recently chased offstage to 'Fetch us in fuel,' 367) emerged to help Prospero dress Miranda in shirt and necklace (to Miranda's obvious discomfort, she 'yanking away ... as though he were collaring her, and biting it, to see if it were edible') before Ferdinand was finally disgorged onto the stage (Rutter 2012: 466).

The montage effect here aligned Caliban's former attempted assault (forgotten or forgiven by Miranda) with Ferdinand's imminent actions, Caliban helping to prepare Miranda for her new suitor. Caliban frequently acted as the transitional figure. Following the attempted murder of Alonso and Gonzalo (2.1), Caliban burst onto the stage and stood amid the nobles as he howled his curse on Prospero (2.2.1–2). Caliban's awareness of the author of his misfortunes threw ironic light on the would-be murderers' ignorance. Later, following Caliban's 'The isle is full of noises' (3.2.135), during which Stephano and Trinculo cowered in fear and clutched at Caliban's legs, the trio's celebratory dance was juxtaposed with the arrival of the exhausted Alonso, Sebastian and Antonio, the temporary joy of the comic rebels undercut by the more physically felt experience of the serious conspirators.

The 'headlining' of transitions also emphasized a recurrent interest in labour. Caliban's calls of 'Hi day, freedom!' (2.2.181) were a much-remarked feature of the company's 1988–9 English-language production, partly for the stir they caused when performed at the Romanian National Theatre in Bucharest during the final year of Ceaușescu's dictatorship; 'Hi day,' as shouted by Duncan Duff's Caliban, was strikingly similar to '*haide*', meaning 'Let's go for it!', and the ensuing tumult brought the company to the attention of the state police (Reade 1991: 80).[8] In the Russian production, as Caliban shouted, the scene paused on the arrival of a staggering Ferdinand, who was carrying a ramrod-straight Ariel on his back. The burdened Ferdinand froze in place as Caliban cried 'freedom!', again offering ironic comment on the new scene. The ensuing 3.1 developed Miranda and Ferdinand's relationship through the visual metaphor of labour (Figure 4). Ferdinand carried Ariel, playing a log, to the far side of the stage and laid him down; Ariel immediately jumped up, walked back to his starting place and lay down again. As Miranda and Ferdinand talked, Ferdinand repeatedly carried Ariel across the stage, first with confidence (including swinging Ariel upside down), then with fatigue (prompting laughter as Ariel looked around quizzically at his slow journey), then by attempting to roll the irritated spirit across the stage, at which Miranda jumped in to help by kicking her father's servant to the end.

As well as being an extraordinary sequence of physical comedy (Kuzichev stayed deadpan as he was subjected to his indignities), the scene opened up consideration of the production's attitude towards state apparatus. Ferdinand laboured Sisyphus-like, while the unfazed Ariel represented the confidence of political power, effortlessly keeping the worker working. When Miranda joined Ferdinand, the two could easily roll Ariel across the stage; but more importantly, the work became less important to them (Ariel tapped his foot impatiently when left too long). As Miranda and Ferdinand swapped names, Ariel looked up at Prospero, who stood atop the wall watching. Through their shared resistance to imposed labour, Miranda and Ferdinand had achieved common purpose, which became the basis of their love. This was followed up in the wedding masque (4.1), refigured as a Bolshevik festival and paean to communist Russia. Black-

FIGURE 4 *Miranda (Anna Khalilulina) and Ferdinand (Yan Ilves). Photograph by Johan Persson/ArenaPAL; www.arenapal.com.*

and-white footage of happy farmers flashed across the back
wall, while three 'goddesses' emerged onto the stage as masked
country girls carrying corn and apples, before giving way
to a dancing chorus of sickle-carrying farmhands. But the
nostalgia was too much for Prospero, who screamed 'Stop' to
halt the music and dancing, then 'Stop!' again to halt the play
itself. The house lights came on, a stagehand entered with a
confused shrug, and an annoyed Ilves went and sat impatiently
in the auditorium. Prospero/Yasulovich finally let his guard
down, addressing 'We are such stuff as dreams are made on'
(4.1.156–7) directly to the audience. As Eleanor Collins puts
it, 'the boundaries between the fiction of performance and its
reality were irrevocably disrupted: the premise of theatrical
narrative itself brought into the spotlight and exposed' (2012:
98). The toppling of even the normative structures of theatre
raised the stakes of Prospero's plan, implying that even the
author had tenuous control of his story.

The rejection of nostalgia was mirrored in a hilarious
rejection also of capitalism, in what Collins calls 'a nod to the
burgeoning consumerism in Russia after the fall of the Soviet
Union' (2012: 98). Caliban, the would-be socialist rebel, led
Trinculo and Stephano to Prospero's cell, only for them to
encounter a projection of a lush boutique shop and displays
of fine clothes, mobile phones and accessories. Trinculo
threw himself with gusto towards the clothes, while Stephano
discovered a credit card and machine with unlimited funds
(Trinculo appeared to orgasm as one of his payments went
through), and the two men then introduced Caliban, their
'"dude" accomplice' (Innes and Shevtsova 2013: 217), to the
joys of paying for goods, the three distracted until Prospero
and his baying hounds entered. In a brilliant conclusion, the
unfazed clowns turned up with shopping bags to the final
reunion, Stephano cheekily calling Trinculo on his new mobile
phone, the nouveau riche confident enough to undermine their
masters.

As ever, though, Cheek by Jowl's primary purpose was
emotional rather than political. The apparent reconciliations

of *The Tempest* were subjected to a series of complications, most notably in the tearing apart of the production's 'greatest discovery' (Innes and Shevtsova 2013: 217) – the close relationship between Caliban and Miranda. As the nobles left, Caliban howled, and Miranda ran back in, crying, and threw herself into Caliban's arms. Ferdinand and Prospero pulled the two apart, and Miranda was carried off flailing and protesting (Collins notes that Ferdinand 'held his hand over her mouth' (2012: 99), a particularly terrifying image in context). Feklistov found that this scene 'made us look into animal instincts of characters' (2016), in a scene that retrospectively informed both of their performances. This final split, however, generated the closing image that healed all wounds. Ariel accepted his freedom quietly and then, after Prospero left, looked about in some confusion. Seeing Caliban rocking gently on the floor, Ariel walked over, sat next to him and put his hand on his head. The shared compassion here implied that, if the play's various splits had not yet been healed, there was at least now the willingness for healing. But the final family portrait, with a defeated and subdued Miranda now quiet at Prospero's feet, closed on an ambiguous freeze-frame that, in the spirit of Truffaut's *The 400 Blows*, pushed interpretation back to the audience, leaving open the future of this visually unified but emotionally scarred group.

Conclusions

Both *Cymbeline* and *The Tempest* staged reunions in their final sequences, and just as Prospero spoke his epilogue to the theatre, so was Posthumus's line 'Live, / And deal with others better' (418–19) addressed to the audience. The return to the theatre, to be 'cheek by jowl' with the audience who provide a touring company's only constant point of reference, is essential to the company's practice, and my utilization of the filmic terminology of cross-cutting, montage and voice-over should not imply the one-sidedness of film presentation. What is most striking about Cheek by Jowl's filmic techniques, in fact, is that they precisely capture the embodied liveness of theatrical performance. Shakespeare's plays operate in linear time – scenes happen in their chronological sequence without the benefit of flashbacks, requiring recapitulation and narrative in order to draw connections between events. Cheek by Jowl's use of frozen and projected subjects, of 'headlining' transitions and montage, all bring bodies *closer together* in space and time. In doing so, Donnellan and Ormerod suggest that what is in a character's mind – whether someone they are thinking about, an action they have committed or an effect they have had – is as real as the person literally in front of them. This also has the effect of undoing the block of time. 'The more we can accept the mastery of Time and resolve to live exclusively in the present, the less we block ourselves' (Donnellan 2005: 227). By collapsing time through overlapping transitions and projected subjects, Donnellan frees the actor to live and respond now.

Cheek by Jowl's actors operate within spaces that, like the film camera, allow the viewer to focus on what is most important. This is also true of the company's approach to the Shakespearean text, respectful but in no way purist. The fast pace, overlapping scenes and intuitive deployment of non-diegetic images in place of long narration all contribute to the filmic aspects of their productions while preserving and indeed enabling the shared occupation of space by figures connected by emotion and consequence. In the next chapter, I move on to two productions with a more complex *mise en scène* and that more explicitly use modern technologies, including those of the camera, but the company's privileging of the actor and the construction of textual, spatial, temporal and scenic worlds around them remain at the heart of Cheek by Jowl's practice.

5

Conceptual rooms: designing not-Shakespeare

'Tis Pity She's a Whore (2011–14) and Ubu Roi (2013–15)

Cheek by Jowl's centring of the actor at the heart of its work has important consequences for the design process. While Donnellan and Ormerod may have ideas about what they want to explore with a company, Donnellan is wary of ideas 'as they tend to come from the head rather than the heart' (2003: 165). The production's look and interpretation instead emerge during rehearsals, rather than from a pre-designed concept. 'Nick does not present a model box on the first day and show costume drawings to a bemused circle of actors who have only just met each other' (Sierz 2010: 153). This is a particular advantage of the Cheek by Jowl framework as opposed to Donnellan and Ormerod's work for other theatres, where a design may be required much earlier in the process, and where 'there is no possibility of modification' once the rehearsal process has begun

(Donnellan 1999: 21; Donnellan and Ormerod 1996: 83). The freedom of the actor to not just be a 'puppet' trapped within *mise en scène* during rehearsals, as Peter Moreton puts it, is essential to the trust and the pleasure of working with Cheek by Jowl: 'there's a freedom you gain from the process, in terms of that there's no rules of what you play in the moment ... there is permission to try things' (2016). This is not to imply that Cheek by Jowl is a democracy; Donnellan describes himself as a 'coach', as distinguished from an acting teacher (Radmall-Quirke 2016). But while Donnellan imposes rules, he is adamant that 'there should be very few rules in rehearsal [and] whenever we seem to be faced with a choice between life or obeying the rule, we should always choose to break the rule. Only life matters. The rest is frivolous' (Donnellan 2018).[1] A pre-designed set, of course, would impose exactly the kinds of constraint that Cheek by Jowl rehearsals are intended to be free of.

Ormerod is unusual among British theatre designers in the consistency of his collaboration with a single director. While both Donnellan and Ormerod have worked separately, the vast majority of their work has been co-created.[2] The partnership is unusual in destabilizing the hierarchy typical of British theatre in which a director chooses a designer for a piece: 'what they are doing is maintaining control of choice, and I'm very lucky in that Declan doesn't have that control' (Ormerod 2002: 5). Ormerod's refreshing philosophy of design privileges space and fluidity over visuals.

The design should support and realise and reveal the piece. But at the same time I feel that you shouldn't come out of any theatre piece, exclaiming 'Oh my God that was a fantastic design. I didn't like the acting or the directing, but I thought the design was fantastic' then I would think that you had failed as a designer ... For example to pretend that you can produce a beautiful set for one scene and not consider how it moves into the next scene is disastrous. You may get some wonderful photographs, but dramatically it's a failure. (Donnellan 2018)[3]

Ormerod, with typical modesty, stresses that the role of the designer is not to promote their own vision but to serve the needs of the production. 'The audience should be able to move completely seamlessly from one scene to the next. And that's a hard thing to do but that's fundamental to the designer's job' (2002: 3). Complex design and set changes would, of course, be antithetical to the overlapping transitions and cross-cutting that characterize Cheek by Jowl's style, and what is often read as a sparseness in Cheek by Jowl's visual style is an artistic choice, freeing the company to get to what is important. This is, of course, also essential to the company's commitment to touring. Cheek by Jowl's records of the company's first fifteen years are dominated by the complex logistical negotiations for shifting a large company from country to country, including costs, weight and visa restrictions, and often carrying set as excess baggage when possible (Cheek by Jowl 1994b). Barbara Matthews notes wryly of a performance of *The Tempest* in Singapore that 'BA lost set – only arrived 4.30pm for 5pm show. They were sponsoring show and took ad in prog. saying "they took pleasure in sponsoring the 'versatile Cheek by Jowl'". Were they trying to prove it??!!!' (Cheek by Jowl 1989c). The company's versatility, including performing without costume or props when necessary (Shaughnessy 2017: 194), is thus born out of a combination of artistic requirement and logistical pragmatism. Ormerod roots this in an idea of 'need':

> From a touring point of view ... things have to be lightweight, but I think there is a more pressing artistic requirement ... I think good design is rooted in need. And that's true of a building, I mean it's true of architecture. You don't build a building with too many columns, you build it with the right number of columns. So that when you look at it you feel as if it stands, and the columns aren't too big or too fat, they're just right according to need. And that's true of the set of a play. I mean, you find an element and it fulfils a need. It may be a need in you as it were, or it may be a need in the piece as realised on stage. (Ormerod 2002: 8)

Cheek by Jowl's economy of design eschews superfluity. The shared creative control allows a perfect marriage of design and direction in which everything on the stage is geared towards the space and predicament of the play, rather than gratuitous spectacle.

As opposed to Cheek by Jowl's early years, when the company played '257 towns in thirty-four different countries' (Prescott 2008: 72) – or, at a local level, twelve different venues in only thirteen days on the *Vanity Fair* tour between 21 November and 3 December 1983 – the company's practice in recent years has involved fewer venues for longer periods, which has allowed them to explore a more elaborate scenic design that nonetheless holds true to the company's ethos of using only what is necessary around the bodies of the actors.[4] In this chapter, I consider productions of two non-Shakespearean plays with Shakespearean roots – John Ford's *'Tis Pity She's a Whore* (2011– 14), which riffs on situations from *Romeo and Juliet*, and Alfred Jarry's *Ubu Roi* (2013–15), which playfully travesties *Macbeth* – whose *mise en scène* conjured a clear, locatable set (respectively, a bedroom and a bourgeois dining room) that remained visible throughout the production. Both locations were inextricably connected with a single young character, respectively Annabella and the anonymous family's son, allowing the productions to concentrate the events of the play around that omnipresent figure. Developing the concepts of produced and frozen subjects explored in the previous chapter, this chapter considers how *mise en scène* allowed Cheek by Jowl to explore further the individual's subjective experience of the space. The desecration of those rooms aligns with the plays' own violent responses to their Shakespearean forebears, making explicit the company's radical reorientation of the spaces of early modern drama.

The bedroom: *'Tis Pity She's a Whore*

As I have noted elsewhere, *'Tis Pity She's a Whore* is repeatedly treated by reviewers as an excessive, taboo-breaking version of *Romeo and Juliet* (Kirwan 2017: 96–7) that converts the forbidden love of Shakespeare's play into an incestuous plot and subjects its characters – particularly its women – to a horrific series of abuses and mutilations as the incest is discovered, culminating in the brother killing his sister and cutting out her heart. Cheek by Jowl's treatment, emphasizing the youth of the couple at the heart of the play's atrocities, was the company's first English-language production since *As You Like It* to go through several iterations and cast changes, including three different Annabellas (Lydia Wilson in 2011/12, Gina Bramhill in 2012/13 and Eve Ponsonby in 2014; my discussion here is drawn from my viewings of the original cast live and on archival video).[5] The production toured extensively in Europe and around the UK, as well as brief visits to the USA and Australia. While the production retained its basic shape and structure, it doubtless shifted substantially with each new Annabella, for the production was literally centred on this young woman's experience – specifically, that which happened in her bed.

Roberta Barker, Kim Solga and Cary Mazer begin their dialogic essay about the production noting that this *"Tis Pity* was resolutely "naturalist" in its set design and its use of offstage spaces; emotional realist in its acting technique; Brechtian in its placement of actors as observers on stage; highly stylized in its use of sound, lighting, dance, and blocking; and "in-yer-face" in its depictions of on and offstage violence' (Barker et al. 2013: 576). The production opened with Annabella lying on a brightly lit bed centre stage. The rest of the set evoked a teenager's bedroom, with red doors and walls covered with posters of classic movies and vampire shows. One door led to an en-suite bathroom, the other a loosely defined 'outside'. The entire play took place within this bedroom, turning it into a public as well as private space, as in the opening sequence. Annabella put on a CD and danced on her bed, hitting the beat hard. As she danced, the rest of the ensemble, wearing their character costumes, danced in, bouncing and clicking their fingers. Counting them in, Annabella synchronized the dancers, and Annabella was joined on the bed by Jack Gordon's Giovanni – who Annabella repeatedly and playfully pushed away – and David Collings's Florio, who watched her closely. After pushing Giovanni away several times, the music suddenly stopped and Giovanni and the Friar (Nyasha Hatendi) launched straight into 1.1 while standing on either side of Annabella's bed.

The opening located the play squarely in Annabella's space, opening up the potential for a feminist reading of a play that repeatedly brutalizes and objectifies its women. The men of the play appeared at first as Annabella's projected subjects, as Dominic Cavendish tentatively suggests: 'It's as if they're spirited into life by Lydia Wilson's Annabella ... whose crimson lair, lined with arty film posters and dominated by a double bed, suggests a cocooned world in which imagination and taboo desire have been allowed to run feverish riot' (2012). Cavendish's remarks suggest a somewhat squeamish attitude towards female sexuality, and at this stage, of course, there was nothing to suggest 'taboo' beyond Annabella's celebration of her own sexuality. But Cavendish rightly identifies that the rest of the play's characters were projected subjects, called into service to allow Annabella – in the safety and privacy of her bedroom – to imagine herself desired, even as she pushed away the projected Giovanni's attentions. Annabella's actions in the opening sequence defined a woman who wanted to *dance*, and who insisted on complete control of her own (and others') bodies.

This was, however, immediately countered by 1.1, which reversed the projection – now Annabella was the projected subject of Giovanni (and, to an extent, the Friar). While the Friar and Giovanni shouted at one another from opposite sides of the bed, Annabella was directly in their eyeline, and Giovanni in particular made no pretence to look at anything else. Annabella was not frozen during this sequence, and remained moving on her bed, initially playing with a sock puppet. In a characteristically playful disregard for spatiotemporal unity, Giovanni interacted with his own projection, regularly joining Annabella on the bed to play with her, arm wrestle, pick her up by the legs. Their play was semi-wrestling, blurring the line between sibling rough play and something more sexual, and the latter intention was made clear both by Giovanni's lust for her and in the Friar's emphatic cries of 'sin' while pointing directly at (and nearly touching) Annabella. This explicit objectifying and judgement of Annabella set up the spatial dynamic of the production that, being orientated around Annabella's bed, epitomized the obsession of the play's men with her sexual availability and activity.

The *mise en scène*, then, elided the distinction between private and public space and, more importantly, between Annabella's subjectivity and her objectification. As Julia Rank argues, 'Displayed as a prize for her parade of suited suitors who prance around her bedroom like male models in a fashion show, she takes the role of a virgin and whore in a series of tableaux moulded by the men who constantly surround her' (Rank 2012); Rank points to the contradiction that the suitors were a parade for Annabella just as Annabella was displayed as a prize for them. The ease with which men 'invaded a teenage girl's bedroom ... was uncomfortable to watch' (Mentz 2012: 323), creating a clear visualization of the liberties that this society took with her body and with her space.

> As the two consummated their mutual love under the red sheets, however, the world closed in on them, in the form of a group of men, including their father, who came on stage to negotiate Annabella's marriage. Having the incestuous affair begin under the not-seeing eyes of the father and his associates may not have been subtle, but the red, moving, audible mass beneath the covers made a potent visible rejoinder to the older men's attempts to control the young woman's body. (Mentz 2012: 323)

Steve Mentz here perfectly captures the complex negotiation of space and entitlement, with the men of the play asserting their proprietary rights over Annabella within the *mise en scène* of her own bedroom, even while the very same *mise en scène* allowed Annabella to assert her own independence of that control under their noses.

Read in this way, it is hard not to see the overall arc of 'Tis Pity as an enactment of male attempts to wrest back agency from Annabella and ensure that their control over her was absolute. From brawls to weddings and murders to confessions, men repeatedly entered and desecrated Annabella's bedroom. As opposed to the productions discussed in Chapters 2 and 3, with their unloaded open space, the detailed set ensured that Annabella's presence was always felt even when Wilson was conceptually or literally offstage. Sometimes this was comic. During 2.2, when Soranzo (Jack Hawkins) fantasized about Annabella, he stepped onto her bed and held out his hand to her, standing her up. He didn't only project his subject, but dramatized her, angling her desk lamp to cast her in divine light. The ensemble joined in, the 'muscle-rippling Adonises' (Collins and Smith 2013: 250) taking off their shirts and holding up halos, drapes and a neon, glowing heart as they gazed up adoringly at her, now a neon Madonna, Soranzo knelt before her in obeisance. While the projection was obviously fantastical, his surrounding and costuming of her with his male attendants also enacted a premature colonization of her bedroom. The disjunction between Soranzo's fantasy and his experience of the real Annabella would be traumatic.

That brutal intrusion of reality happened quickly; as Catherine Silverstone puts it, 'while he might be able to see his own desire in the body of Annabella, Soranzo is unable to read Annabella's desire from her body' (2010: 83). With 4.2 cut, 4.1 and 4.3 overlapped, moving seamlessly from wedding to wedding night. Hippolyta (Suzanne Burden) ended the previous scene choking to death on the bed while Annabella mopped the dying woman's forehead; in the overlapping transition, Hippolyta was not yet dead as Soranzo called his wife 'famous whore' (4.3.1). Soranzo's sudden, real presence in Annabella's teenage bedroom made her shift in status acute, her self-expressed sexuality suddenly exchanged for Soranzo's objectifying, oblivious gaze. The fact that Soranzo held a knife ahead of undressing her, and pulled down her wedding dress to leave her in veil, gloves and underwear, only underscored the one-sided control, as if Annabella was suddenly being forced to play Soranzo's projected version of herself. Only now the projection was not playing along, she was stiff, unresponsive and inscrutable.

In this sequence, the male concern for Annabella's sexual availability – hitherto implicitly scrutinized by the men who invaded her bedroom space – became explicit, firstly in Soranzo stripping her. As Donnellan suggests, the company's first production of the play in 1980 'was about a religious patriarchy dominating women ... [but] the second time, I thought it was about women who transgress. Every single one of the women transgresses and they get punished outrageously by the men for so doing' (Donnellan and Ormerod 2016). In an inspired reinterpretation of the text, Soranzo began the scene playfully; it was only during the course of undressing her that he realized she was pregnant, and she treated his shock with scornful defiance. Soranzo vacillated between devastation and rage, his violence a response to his embarrassed failure to read Annabella's body correctly. Instead of threatening to kill her, he grabbed her by the hair and forced her offstage into the bathroom, then returned to the bedroom to grab a wire hanger. It was the intervention of Vasques (Laurence Spellman), arriving and interrupting the impromptu abortion, which rescued Annabella.

The threat of enforced abortion was a climactic moment of violation that aligned the set with the young woman's body. Having shifted from Madonna to whore in Soranzo's eyes, he assumed complete possession of her body and her space. Vasques's intervention deferred this action; as Soranzo and Annabella returned to the bedroom, Annabella wrapped herself in her duvet while Soranzo curled up in a more subservient position on the floor. Under Vasques's influence, Soranzo's subsequent approach of love and guilt left Annabella emotionally and physically exposed; she emerged from under the duvet and teetered back and forth before him, until he covered her with a shirt and embraced her. The emotional manipulation here bears out Ben Brantley's observation that the pity of this production is 'that she hasn't been given the time and space to figure out who she is' (2012); unable to adjust to Soranzo and Vasques's machinations, Annabella became pliant. His change of tack allowed Soranzo to finally remove Annabella from the bedroom for the first time in the production, leaving Vasques free to completely occupy the space for his acts of violent mutilation against her maid.

Vasques's abuse of Lizzie Hopley's Putana was especially traumatic. Voyeur-like, he stood unobserved watching Putana flit about the room, looking sadly at the dishevelled bed and helping herself to chocolates. She 'desperately longed to recapture her mistress's youthful radiance' (Collins and Smith 2013: 250), trying on Annabella's school skirt and tie. Vasques took advantage of her loneliness, coming forward to flirt with her, and she giggled in enjoyment of her naughtiness. But then, a doorbell rang and they were joined by a stripper (Jimmy Fairhurst), who jumped onto the bed and began dancing. The violation of Annabella's space was completed as Putana threw herself into the party, sandwiched between Vasques and his henchman and taking drugs pulled out of the stripper's jockstrap. In the throes of her recaptured youth, she announced that Annabella was carrying Giovanni's baby. Pausing to reflect on the news, Vasques signalled to the stripper, who pinned Putana down on the bed and kissed her until she began thrashing; finally, her assailant threw his head back to spit out the tongue he had bitten from her mouth. The murderer wrapped his belt around his fist and dragged his gagging victim into the bathroom, closing the door. 'For the second time,' notes Stéphane Huet, 'the bathroom is used as a space where traces of crimes can be washed away. Yet the director does not provide the murderers with an easy escape' (2012: 17). When it opened again, it was to reveal a 'hallucinatory hell' (McNulty 2013) in which green mist and a chorus of screaming figures, the results of Soranzo's jealousy, spilled onto the stage.

The dragging of the two women between bedroom and bathroom (as Kim Solga points out, 'the most intimate of spaces' (Barker et al. 2013: 578)), drew attention to the alignment between sexual activity and bodily functions, and between two different kinds of private space that emphasized the play's violations against women. Mazer imagined 'the bed functioning as a "target" in Donnellan's sense of the term ... [which] allows him to retain Stanislavsky's focus on emotional action *without* allowing the actors to get hung up in Strasbergian introspection' (Barker et al. 2013: 578). More importantly, however, the bed served as a metonym for Annabella itself. The bed externalized a range of drives and impulses, especially the desire to *possess* or *occupy* the woman, and thus the bed; control of the bed space equated to control of Annabella herself. As Donnellan notes, 'The target is always active ... is always doing something' (Donnellan 2005: 24); actions could be conceptualized in terms of *what could be done* to the bed, the repeated site of activity and violation. The upstage bathroom, on the other hand, retained some mystery and privacy, its offstage status allowing for naturalistic aural evocations of body horror.

Yet despite the overt desecrations of Annabella's space by Soranzo and Vasques, the most damaging intrusions were those that initially seemed welcome – Giovanni's. From the opening image of Annabella playfully pushing Giovanni away, there had been an implied resistance to her brother's takeover, a negotiation of the terms on which he was allowed in. Throughout, Giovanni assumed a privilege that allowed him to join her projection on the bed, to film her during the wedding sequence, to enter freely; but Annabella resisted more overtly his final entrance during Soranzo's birthday party (5.5). Giovanni joined her on the bed and tried to touch her, but she pulled away, resisting his attempts to hold her down. She tried to run from the room, at which he picked her up, brought her back to the bed and laid her down. Annabella's attempt to leave the room of her own volition was another rarity for the production, she seeming to attempt to escape herself at a moment of crisis. Giovanni took off his shirt and straddled her while she shouted at him; he spoke of killing her and she screamed, a scream he stifled with a kiss (evoking the image of the stripper kissing Putana on the same bed). Crucially, the moment of her killing was delayed past its point in the text. She pulled away from him and spoke her final line, 'Farewell, / Brother, unkind' (5.5.92–3) as a final attempt to repossess her space. He responded by suddenly snapping her neck. Annabella was left looking out at the audience, an expression of shock on her face, before her body crumpled onto the bed in what Orlando James (Giovanni in the revivals) describes as a 'pin drop' moment (2016).

Roberta Barker notes her uncertainty about whether the production had an objective reality or whether it was all taking place in Annabella's head; but, as she notes, 'even if it did happen objectively, the action was clearly shaped by Annabella's imagination, rather than by Giovanni's; her wishes, her choices, drove the action much more than his did' (Barker et al. 2013: 583). As this chapter has argued, I suspect neither option entirely encompasses the spatial and temporal complexity of the production's multiple overlapping projected subjects. Certainly, once her spirit left her body, there was no sense in which this was still happening in Annabella's head, and I am inclined to see Wilson's performance as negotiating brilliantly the multiple complex identities of the teenaged woman, whether 'genuine', projected, self-constructed or externally determined. At this point, however, as Giovanni drew a heart on his bare torso in lipstick before carrying her body into the bathroom, the production shifted to his point of view. Mazer notes that the bathroom, having been used for acts of douching, excreting and showing,

> is also the place where Giovanni, with the door closed, dismembers Annabella's body ... Giovanni (among others) wants to see inside Annabella's body; that is the conceit that powers the entire play, if not early modern tragedy in general. And the bathroom's naturalistic semi-transparency, especially as he hacks up her body, articulates beautifully the mad futility of that (entirely naturalistic) ambition. (Barker et al. 2013: 580)

In the production's final moments, the graphic naturalism of the bathroom re-entered the space of the bed, as Giovanni brought out Annabella's heart and sat with it on the bed, to the shock of everyone at the party. Soranzo ran to the bathroom, revealing it to be covered in blood, while others collapsed and shrieked. Then, as sirens grew louder in the background, Annabella herself re-emerged, coming close to the near-catatonic Giovanni and reaching out for her own heart. The production went to blackout on the final image of the dead woman reversing her final journey, moving from the graphic place of execution to the bed with which she had been identified throughout the production, and that now was visibly associated with her own heart.

If Giovanni did want to see inside Annabella's own heart, he might have simply looked around the bedroom that expressed her personality and independence. But of course, Giovanni's actual impulse wasn't to see inside her heart, but to possess it: an image he finally achieved, graphically, removing her body from the space so that he could occupy it unchallenged. Yet his slippage into a form of madness, and Annabella's projected reappearance, made clear that, just like the set itself, Annabella could never be definitively removed from this room. Just as the men of Ford's world had focused all of their energies onto invading Annabella's space and ultimately taking it over, so could they never rid themselves of her. At the end of this production, with the Cardinal's final titular words pointedly left unspoken, Annabella was the only one left moving: the only one who, paradoxically, still seemed to be alive in a room of her own.

The dining room: *Ubu Roi*

If Annabella was the victim of men invading her space, then the protagonist of *Ubu Roi* (2013–15) revelled in the opportunity to invade someone else's. Alfred Jarry's 1896 play, which riffs on *Macbeth*, is described by its translators as 'a preposterous farce, an anarchic parody, an energetically violent and scatological gesture against propriety, smugness, and stupidity in general, as well as against the tame theatrical conventions of its time' (Keith and Legman 2003: v).[6] It is a notoriously difficult play to stage, but Cheek by Jowl's approach made revolutionary sense of the play by foregrounding its 'gesture against propriety,' utilizing another unusually detailed *mise en scène* and an elaborate framing device to, as with *'Tis Pity*, place a single ever-present figure – here, a teenage boy – at the centre of the chaos.

Speaking ahead of the live webstream of a performance at the Brooklyn Academy of Music, Donnellan responded to the received wisdom that Jarry's play is a schoolboy's scatological diatribe against a hated teacher, arguing that 'Although Jarry thought he was writing about his schoolteacher, the more you read the play, it's not about a schoolteacher, it's about a mother and a father' (Donnellan and Ormerod 2015). Ormerod took over: 'we see the action through Alfred Jarry himself as a young boy ... we go into his life in a modern apartment and we take him through the story, and in leaps between his parents giving a party for some sophisticated guests, and then in one leap he goes into this scatological world.' While credited as Bougrelas, therefore, I refer to Sylvain Levitte's character in this production as 'Jarry', the creative team's avatar for the playwright himself. Here, however, Jarry's weapon was not a pen and exercise book, but a camcorder, with which the teenage boy scrutinized his parents, their friends and the bourgeois environment of their too-pristine apartment.

As with *'Tis Pity, Ubu Roi* opened with a youth alone on stage, here a boy (Levitte) reclining on a sofa. Clearly, though, this was not the boy's space. Ormerod's modern apartment was white – white panels, with doors set into the wall; a blank fireplace and mantel, bland white paintings. Jarry lay on a plush white sofa, behind a white, glass-topped coffee table holding an ice bucket and nibbles. A dining table, laid for a dinner party, was at the far end of the stage. The whiteness was not clinical, but sterile, and the boy looked distinctly uncomfortable. Just as his own Action Man-style toy, sat on the coffee table next to the ice bucket, was a disruption to the formal cleanliness of the apartment, so did Jarry himself risk appearing as a messy presence in this 'asphyxiating, sterile' little world (Cavendish 2015b).

In a long, near-silent opening sequence, Jarry began filming the set, establishing the fine details of the space that would shortly be destroyed. First, he filmed his own face, and the image was projected live onto the back wall, adding colour and movement to the anaemic facade (Figure 5). Then he began filming the room's objects, zooming in excruciatingly close on flowers, matches, a remote control. He wandered upstage and through the stage right door into a kitchen. Momentarily breaking the feed, the now-empty stage was dominated by the live video feed, which showed pre-recorded scenes of the rest of the apartment. Jarry's camera initially captured the mundane preparations of his Mother (Camille Cayol) and Father (Christophe Grégoire) for a dinner party, but as it lingered, it captured more disturbing detail: the slight bend in the tomatoes as they were sliced, the interior of his father's nostrils, the individual hairs on his mother's fur coat. As soon as the camera got too close, everything in this refined apartment became horrific. In a particularly unsettling moment, he entered his parents' bedroom, focusing first on the sheets and then on a lipstick mark on a glass of water. In the perfectly white bathroom, he scanned the toilet until he found the tiniest smear of shit on the seat and a urine stain on the rug, stains that symbolized 'the dark hidden part of such polite people' (Vallejo 2013) and were blown up on screen to dominate the living room.

Ormerod's design was based on the Parisian apartment where he and Donnellan were staying, which 'looked so beautiful, it was like a trap ... We were told that we couldn't cut anything on the surfaces in the kitchen, and we couldn't have more than one guest in ... you couldn't walk on the floor before eight o'clock or after eleven o'clock ... you couldn't use

FIGURE 5 *Jarry/Bougrelas (Sylvain Levitte). Photograph by Johan Persson/ArenaPAL; www.arenapal.com.*

the kitchen counter … the flush couldn't be pulled before a certain time' (Donnellan and Ormerod 2016). The pre-recorded scenes were filmed in that flat, which Donnellan described as producing an 'incredible effect in me and Nick' that translated into the desire to smash and destroy: 'if we're given the right space we will just regress.' This was coupled with Donnellan and Ormerod's own recollections of an excruciating dinner party, 'constipated within an inch of its life', that produced a similar 'Ubu effect'. Ralf Remshardt describes the play as an 'intertextual grotesque' that operated a 'scorched-earth policy towards the pieties of nineteenth-century drama and nineteenth-century art' (2004: 175); the Ubu effect excited in Donnellan and Ormerod resulted in a production built around a similar policy towards bourgeois niceties.

Party and set together informed the primary *études* in pre-rehearsals for *Ubu*, which reunited an ensemble who had all worked with Donnellan and Ormerod on *Andromaque* (2007).[7] The *études* were designed to explore the idea that, as opposed to being a framing device, 'the main play is in the bourgeois family story, and inside of this Ubu appears' (Boiffier 2016). The actors simply improvised chit-chat:

> They had to do their biographies for us ... I pretended to be another sort of director and actually interviewed them in their characters. I tried to be earnest and humourless. They just had to be as boring as possible ... they had to behave as dinner guests who would stop at nothing to achieve consensus. So they'd get marks for saying things like '*what sort of wine do you prefer?*' '*Well, if it's meat I prefer red wine, but on the whole if it's fish I go for white*' ... And they had to keep this conversation going on forever. They couldn't let the energy flag. They had to share the chat equally, with charm and elegance and smiles. We used to listen to them for hours, and the terrible thing is, it was much funnier than anything Jarry ever wrote – it was excruciatingly funny. I threatened terrifying punishments if they ever laughed and even worse punishments if they ever made the audience laugh. They had to be just inaudible, like people at the next table. What was bizarre was that everything they said was hilarious. And the more boring they tried to be the more we were all in stitches. And the most work was done on getting them to improvise the world's most boring dinner party without laughing. It was different every night. I think they were all so scared of laughing that it gave a lot of edge! (Donnellan and Ormerod 2016)

As Cécile Leterme puts it, 'he asked us to invent, to improvise, the bourgeois part of the text. And so we worked on how to keep it really low stakes, no stakes at all: very smooth, very polite and open, no introspection at all – very smooth, uninteresting, absolutely uninteresting' (2016). In the final production, as the three guests arrived, welcomed with polite laughs from their hosts, the work of the *études* manifested in the incessant mumble of meaningless chatter, the banality of this bourgeois dinner party capturing the stifling constriction that had prompted such a visceral desire to misbehave in Donnellan and Ormerod. Jarry's scatological eruptions didn't just grow out of this environment – they smashed into it, tore it apart.

The first overt indication of the production's intentions came as the Mother and Father made the finishing touches to their party clothes. As the two helped each other dress and the Father reached out to touch the Mother, Jarry sat bolt upright on the sofa. Pascale Noel's lighting snapped to a green wash, and a screeching note pierced the soundscape. The Mother and Father were thrown apart, and started jerking, adopting the disjointed, jagged movements that would distinguish Mère and Père Ubu from the Mother and Father. All elbows and knees, the two writhed in contorted, abstract shapes, a release of 'that crazy energy of what's going on underneath' (Gibson 2016). The first instance of this lasted for only a few seconds, but it happened twice more, always when the Father went to put his hands on the Mother. Young Jarry's Freudian obsession with his parents' sexuality, with the venality that underlay the stifling formality on the surface, generated the nightmarish world of the Ubus, drawing on the horror of *grand guignol* and Claude Chabrol (Leterme 2016).

This violent shift in the performance environment importantly did not affect the set in any way; indeed, the continued visibility of the dining room and its accoutrements was essential to decoding the meaning of what followed. Noel's lighting design and Jane Gibson's movement direction created a different performance-scape that allowed the two worlds to exist on top of one another, constantly foregrounding the actions of the Ubus as Jarry's projection of what underlay the dinner party. As Donnellan told the cast, 'it's not a framing device, it's a play *about* the dinner party, and every now and then there's an eruption into this play that takes over, but then you go back. So it's not the frame – the painting is the dinner party' (Donnellan and Ormerod 2016). What was left beautifully ambiguous was the precise nature of what young Jarry was uncovering in his projected fantasies: how far 'the whole ghastly sequence [was] a teenage take on, a myth-making around, the awfulness of the adults around him' (Dunnett 2013), and how far the interactions between the characters of *Ubu* shed light on what really underlay the bourgeois pretensions of his parents and their friends.

Young Jarry found the world of the Ubus far more stimulating than the dinner party, regularly filming the action with an expression of delicious glee on his face, while happy to at first remain an observer. As the Ubus took over, 'with laugh-out-loud switches of intensity, between the babble of an ordinary bourgeois private function and the madly caricatured epic misadventures of the royal pair' (Taylor 2013), they proceeded to systematically destroy the living room through misuse and misappropriation of everything from kitchen tools to furniture, much as Annabella's bedroom had been misused in *'Tis Pity*; here, however, the destruction was both liberating and terrifying. A crucial distinction between the two worlds was that the actors moved about the set in anything *but* a genteel, appropriate fashion when playing the Ubus. In his first appearance as fellow conspirator Bordure (1.3), Xavier Boiffier entered from the stage left door and plastered himself to the back wall, edging along it, while Mère and Père did the same from the opposite direction, evoking a two-dimensional shadow puppet show, choreographed with the near-stop motion of German expressionist silent cinema. Bordure creeped towards the Ubus like Nosferatu, while the Ubus leaned obliquely towards him as their alliance literally came together. Elsewhere in the production, the cast moved in strange and unexpected directions; encouraged by Gibson to 'use the diagonals' (Leterme 2016), they walked over rather than around the sofa and table, ran in zigzags and crawled painstakingly along the carpets.

Equally disruptive was the mess that the characters started causing. As Mère wooed Bordure in 1.3 with talk of the menu, Cayol repeatedly ran into the kitchen and back out with bags of salad and boxes of cornflakes, and threw them in Bordure's general direction, beginning the process of redistributing the apartment among the Ubus's world. The Ubus lay flat on the floor among the discarded food as they cemented their alliance, lying in rather than consuming the food, thus establishing the production's perverse language of misuse. Much of the production's humour came from the inventive ways in which almost everything onstage was appropriated to serve the needs of the Ubus's world. On Wenceslas's first entrance (1.6), he was 'crowned' by Jarry with a lampshade from a table lamp and held a pepper grinder and ice bucket as his mace and sceptre. Later, Ubu armed himself with a toilet brush, and a broom became Bougrelas's sword of destiny. Despite the unusually complex *mise en scène*, then, the production epitomized Ormerod's earlier statement that the 'essence of theatre is paring down to the essentials of what you actually need: cutting it back until you discover what you need, and maybe that one thing serves many different functions which is theatrical in itself' (Donnellan and Ormerod 1996: 86). Objects that earlier seemed trivial suddenly became gloriously, inappropriately, practical.

The irreverent utilization of the set provided a constant comic underscoring to the Ubu scenes, with an inventive cruelty that might be compared to the opening sequence of Julie Taymor's *Titus* (1999), in which a child also uses foodstuffs and kitchen implements in violent creative play that gets quickly out of hand. The assassination of Wenceslas (2.2) was a case in point, with Père plunging an electric whisk through Wenceslas's (Vincent de Bouard) lampshade to mangle his victim's brains. The comic grotesquery (with de Bouard gibbering and rolling his eyes) added an extraordinary viciousness to the act, delighting in the gyrating of the King's body and the incongruity of the murder weapon, but also highlighted the macabre practicality of this Ubu. The violence repeatedly transcended the different stage worlds – when Père later gouged out Bordure's eye, he used copious ketchup and a small tomato to stand for the eye; that eye was later, in a transition back to the dinner party, popped back into the salad bowl.

While the Ubus desecrated the stage, Jarry cast himself as Bougrelas. Unlike the others, Bougrelas moved relatively naturalistically, with something of a swashbuckling heroic gait as he squirted kitchen cleaner into the faces of his assailants following the initial murder, then escorted his mother the Queen (Leterme) to safety and wept over her as she died in his arms. The son imagined himself as hero, on equal terms with the adults and able to resist both the abstracted physicality and the comic grotesquery of their fantastical versions. In a particularly delightful moment in 2.5, he swore vengeance as he wielded the sword of destiny '*in an attitude of ecstasy*' (26), but behind him the lights of the 'real' world came back up and the guests resumed chatting politely to one another. While Jarry/Bougrelas went through slow-motion actions of thrusting his sword, licking the blood from it and conquering his enemies, the guests ignored him, rendering his actions mere childish play and momentarily foregrounding the extent to which he was lost in his own projected fantasy.

The playful slippage between the two worlds unsettled the barriers of performance, with Jarry/Bougrelas far from the only one whose performance slipped between the production's two worlds. For the infamous set piece of 3.2, the newly crowned Père carried out a series of executions of nobles, judges and financiers.[8] Each terrified group was brought in gibbering from the upstage left door and made to stand before Père, who put a large laundry bag over their heads and shepherded them as a group into the kitchen, from where were heard 'the screams of the off-stage waste disposal unit' (Fernandez 2013). Père then staggered back out, hung up a bloody apron and repeated the sequence while an increasingly drunken Mère reeled about the stage. During the third iteration, however, even as he toyed with the financiers, the green wash of the Ubus's world suddenly returned to the soft light of the dinner party, and the financiers became the mumbling dinner party guests again, even while the bag remained on their heads. Père, meanwhile, suddenly saw the audience. In a boundary-breaking reimagining of the famous 'down the trap' sequence that is regularly made local, Père grabbed the laundry bag, staggered forward and fell off the edge of the stage. At the BAM performance, he switched into English and called out for more volunteers, particularly asking for bankers, rich people and real estate moguls, before asking the audience how he would do in the primaries. The deliberate shattering of spatial distinctions – first in Père remaining as Père while the others reverted to the dining room, and then his invasion of the auditorium – saw the production at its most dangerous as it promised, as with Yasulovich's Prospero (Chapter 4), a character whose control of the theatrical reality could explode from the *mise en scène*.

The blurred lines between the overlapping theatrical worlds rendered the whole production one long transition, with all subjects simultaneously 'real' and projected, and both psychic and physical space manipulated to express individual experience. When the dinner party resumed, the set remained destroyed, the detritus of the Ubus's perversions making visible the underpinning chaos. As Michael Billington puts it, 'Ormerod's set, incorporating battlefield chaos in a world of civilised chic, reinforces the point that murderous monstrosity, as with charity, begins at home' (2013). The dual perspective kept the stakes as high as possible, even while rendering massacres a domestic banality; 'no sooner have we seen the father filmically committing an act of unspeakable torture than his wife breezes into the dining room asking, "Anyone allergic to pine nuts?"' (Billington 2013). Jarry/Bougrelas saw both worlds simultaneously, his righteous anger informing his revulsion in both worlds. His role as cameraman similarly crossed over, as well as creating new spaces within the living room environment, as when conspirators gathered behind the sofa or under the dining table to be filmed whispering in extreme close up. The camera became both Jarry's main expression of agency, as he chose what to document, and latterly his weapon.

As Jarry/Bougrelas filmed, his fantasy became increasingly uncomfortable. Act 3, scene 1 was played as a sex scene, the distinction between Père/Mère and Jarry's parents disappearing as Jarry filmed them having sex in extreme close up. As the two talked, their actions became more grotesque, including Père licking Mère's hands and then her foot, dribbling spittle all over it and then waggling his tongue up and down her ankle, the camera gazing unflinchingly. Père ended this sequence by hitting Mère in the darkness, and Jarry filmed his mother closely as she sobbed quietly. This scene – a loose reimagining of Macbeth dismissing Lady Macbeth once in power – took on a fresh dimension when seen through the eyes of Mère's protective son, and the confrontation between Père and Bougrelas was clearly informed by it. As the war began, the first fight saw Bougrelas throwing things at Père from a distance, and Père responding by suddenly, and with the smooth movements that characterized the Father rather than Père, slapping Bougrelas and pushing him down. Without the normal markers of transitions between worlds, they had suddenly become father and son again, and the soldiers had reverted to embarrassed dinner guests, watching their host take his teenage son in hand.

Jarry/Bougrelas took his final revenge in a compressed version of Act 5. As Père and Mère reunited under an upturned sofa, Père held his wife down while Bougrelas, unseen, held a gun on him. Watching, Bougrelas suddenly shot his gun into the air, and the stage plunged into darkness, before Bougrelas turned on his camera's light. With the stage lit only by this single beam, Bougrelas shot Mère in the head. The screen, capturing the camera's gaze down the gun barrel, became a first-person shooter as the teenager acted out his fantasies by chasing down the other adults, trapping them in the camera's glare and gunning them down, until finally Père fell while trying to scale the back wall of the room. All that was left was the light of the camera, sweeping the audience. Then, the lights of the dinner party came back up, with the diners enjoying a final course of wine and cheese. Jarry, looking a little bereft and sheepish, tidied himself up, mussed his hair, then went and finally joined the adults at the table, helping himself to some cheese as the lights went down.

The sudden, violent culmination of the boy's fantasies, realized in a terrifyingly brutal series of executions, allowed for many potential interpretations. Had the production revealed that the repressed violence of this world informed the actions and desires of the youth as much as it underscored those projected onto the adults? Or had the boy achieved some kind of catharsis and was now able to put aside childish things and begin participating in polite society? Whatever the seeming peace of the cheese and wine, the diners were still surrounded by the debris and mess of the Ubus's macabre pleasures and perverse destruction. Ultimately, it was the set that carried the weight of meaning, the whiteness of the apartment thoroughly and seemingly irreparably destroyed.

Conclusions

In my view, the designer (in collaboration with the director) defines the space. The act of theatre is essentially a willing conspiracy between actor and audience – one performing feats of the imagination, the other suspending their disbelief – that begins when the houselights dim, and finishes when the cast take their final bow. This is only possible with clear rules. That's where the designer comes in, creating a physical and imaginative space for both actors and audience to inhabit. (Ormerod 2009)

The physical and imaginative space of these complex productions, which required audiences to simultaneously decode a detailed set and overlook the breaking of naturalistic rules, marked an exciting evolution in Cheek by Jowl's integration of bodies and design. This space was never empty of semiotic markers; the owners of the depicted rooms – Annabella in 'Tis Pity, the Mother and Father in *Ubu* – were ever-present through the extension of their own personalities into the design. The attacks on these spaces were attacks on the characters who they represented, with the attackers attempting to imprint their own identities and unleash their unspoken desires on each other, raising the stakes for the central figures.

In defining the space, Ormerod and Donnellan extended the subjective impulses of their characters into *mise en scène*, as perhaps most apparent in the use of video cameras in both. Giovanni's regular filming of Annabella throughout evoked a *Peeping Tom*-style obsession with his sister in his need to capture her, a form of control that aligned ideologically with his final colonization of the bed and his sister's body. The motif was logically extended in *Ubu Roi* by inviting the audience to see what Jarry saw as he first anatomized then framed his victims before finally weaponizing his camera. Both cameramen were the last ones standing at the ends of their fictions, ultimately privileging their view. Yet the set exerted a powerful counter-influence that re-produced the subjects whose identities they embodied: Jarry was reintegrated into the dining room despite its destruction, and Annabella returned to her bed to reclaim her own heart from Giovanni. The complex interactions of body and a clearly defined set made explicit the extent to which participants and their environment are mutually complicit in the management and destruction of space, a pattern that holds true across Cheek by Jowl's productions of Shakespeare plays when the environment is often less visible, but no less constructed and deconstructed by its inhabitants.

6

Empathy and loneliness

Much Ado about Nothing (1998) and Measure for Measure (2013–)

On 29 July 2016, Declan Donnellan was awarded the Golden Lion of Venice for lifetime achievement at the Biennale Festival. The citation justified the award

> for his profound faith in the text. For his ability to bring classic works to life for a contemporary audience, without ever losing the ability to 'read' them. For placing actors at the heart of his work and managing to get the very best out of them. When talking about productions by Declan Donnellan, one is talking about extraordinary endeavours in the field of acting. (Baker 2016)

It is revealing that, in line with how Donnellan talks about his own work, the citation does not mention the word 'directing'. Donnellan refers to himself as a director, but that 'directing in a more traditional sense, "Move down stage a bit," or "can we light this bit?" … is way down the line for me' (Sierz 2010: 158). The language of enabling and coaching recurs more often: 'one of [the director's functions] is to look after the health of the acting of the ensemble. In other words, not only to help the actors to act, but to help the actors to act together and to help the actors to act with the audience' (Donnellan 2009: 71), not teaching but removing the blocks that impede the actors' aliveness in the space. In his acceptance speech for the Golden Lion Award, Donnellan focused on the idea of empathy:

> When we put on a piece of theatre we are a group of people looking at other people doing something, and that really couldn't be more important. It's very important politically. We're facing very frightening times, and we need to develop our empathy. And the best way to develop our empathy is to make a sharp distinction between that and our sympathy … 'I feel the same as you'. This is the complete opposite of empathy, by my definition. Empathy is understanding we have no idea what the other person is feeling. (Donnellan 2016)

Donnellan's call for empathy, as he went on to expound in his speech, extends to those with whom he disagrees profoundly and viscerally, whether Brexiteers or Trump supporters, because 'the best way for them to rise is for the rest of us to say that they are either stupid or evil. We need to have an empathetic connection to understand … to see that another human being is different from me is the first act of any political discussion' (2016). At the heart of Donnellan's philosophy is the insistence that everyone is human, and that change – and theatre – come from the understanding that other people are different to me.

In Cheek by Jowl's practice, this philosophy leads to productions of unusual moral and emotional complexity. There are no simple villains or clowns, no unambiguous happy endings or binary black/white dichotomies. Cheek by Jowl's concept, such as it is, is to treat characters as humans with stakes, and thus to allow something 'alive' to emerge.

This aspect of Cheek by Jowl's work has to be considered holistically, and so in this final chapter, I apply the principles of the previous chapters to two of the company's most thoughtful and surprisingly emotional productions. *Much Ado about Nothing* (1998) was the final production of the company's 'Act One' before Ormerod and Donnellan's sabbatical.[1] *Measure for Measure* (2013–present) was the company's second production of the play, this time in Russia in its first collaboration with Moscow's Pushkin Theatre, with many of the regular Russian ensemble players on board. Both productions, nominally comedies, combined hilarious moments with quiet sobriety, resulting in reflective explorations of the gender dynamics of the love plots and a rare attention to loneliness.

Much Ado about Nothing

The word 'sad' and its derivative forms appear more often in *Much Ado about Nothing* than in any other Shakespeare play; for all its comic reputation, its characters spend a great deal of time reflecting on their own melancholy.[2] As Erin Sullivan argues, it is a play that particularly 'depicts this struggle between painful passion and rational counsel … highlighting the difficulty, even hypocrisy of rationalizing away a debilitating sorrow' (2013: 175). The predilection for productions of *Much Ado about Nothing* that stress the play's comic aspects, particularly through slapstick comedy (Benedick being electrocuted in a Christmas tree during 2.3 in Christopher Luscombe's 2015 RSC production, or dive-bombing into a swimming pool in Nicholas Hytner's 2007 National Theatre version, for instance), and focus on the witty banter between Beatrice and Benedick often overshadows the play's constant references to melancholy and passion. Cheek by Jowl, by contrast, foregrounded the sadness. The ensemble marched on stage at the top of the production, walking in lines as they gave a spirited rendition of 'Sigh no more' (2.3.60ff), which culminated in a sudden freeze on the stressed line 'Converting all your sounds of woe' (66).[3] It was the 'sounds of woe' that lingered over the opening lines of 1.1 announcing the approach of Don Pedro, his army and especially Claudio, establishing a tonal quality that would pervade the production and undermined the performed joviality of the arriving army.

In the vein of the company's other 1990s productions of early modern plays, the stage was largely bare but with long, white drapes upstage descending from the flies. The company were richly dressed in period costume: 'end of 19th century, in and around a country house in the south of England' (Cheek by Jowl 1998), a popular period setting for the play since John Barton's 1976 RSC production (Cox 1997: 74). Here, the *mise en scène* evoked the polite society of the English upper-middle classes, with the military element foregrounded in the men's immaculate green uniforms and sashes, and the domestic element captured in the delicate tea service provided on their return from the wars. As Ormerod notes,

> *Much Ado about Nothing* played in costumes of the Boer war period. The period released the language. We worked with Joan Washington on dialect, and we had one session when the sense of the military in the play was totally realised by giving it a military, pre-First World War voice. It made the language immediately comprehensible. (Donnellan 2018)[4]

The setting here allowed for an exploration of the formal, occasionally passive-aggressive, often repressed interactions of its characters, and what Anna Kamaralli brilliantly articulates as 'the destructive aspects of male bonding, that rendered the women marginal and struggling to register their experience as important' (2012: 114). In particular, Beatrice and Benedick's negotiations as they came to terms with their own issues as well as each other offered a nuanced reading of their relationship.

Matthew Macfadyen's Benedick was a deeply conflicted figure from the start. He first appeared as a frozen subject while a messenger announced the army's return. When the honour newly bestowed on Claudio was announced (1.1.10), a roar from the soldiers introduced them as a brash collective, hoisting Claudio on their shoulders. The establishment of male camaraderie was essential in contextualizing the play's male–male relationships, as Macfadyen describes:

It's an environment where men are allowed to love each other completely, not amorous love but total love. Because they're saving each other's lives every day, or they would die for each other, literally. And they're in a terribly difficult, high stakes environment. But there's a great comfort in that. And all of them say they'd go back there, to this really desperate place ... we were talking about this with the soldiers who come back – there's a culture, there's that thing that's very safe. (2016)

The safe space of the military was shown through the men's physical confidence with one another as they fell into play-fighting. Their camaraderie was undermined by Beatrice (Saskia Reeves) walking in front of the group as she spoke dismissively of Benedick (1.1.28ff); the group froze in undignified positions, broken up by short bursts of noise as Benedick wrestled with Claudio (Bohdan Puraj), pinning his friend to the floor. Yet when the soldiers finally arrived, Benedick was clearly uncomfortable. Beatrice barely welcomed him, and Benedick stood awkwardly, speaking with a sharp military clip as if unsure what to do with himself in this domestic environment.

Yet Benedick also quickly became isolated from his military colleagues. When Claudio broached the subject of Hero with him, Benedick guffawed loudly at his own jokes about Hero's stature, to Claudio's obvious discomfort. When Benedick realized Claudio was serious, however, they both lapsed into silence before Benedick burst out in anger 'Is't come to this?' (1.1.186). Benedick then tried to joke about Claudio with Pedro (Stephen Mangan), but Pedro took Claudio's request seriously. Benedick was left isolated centre stage, his remarks and presence unwelcome; following a gesture from Claudio, he wandered away in defeat. This unusually sober, if not bitter, Benedick was in some ways indistinguishable from Paul Goodwin's Don John, the two malcontent and ill at ease in a social setting. This likeness was emphasized by the transition between 1.3 and 2.1, in which Beatrice and Ursula (who took Antonio's lines throughout) reflected on John's 'melancholy disposition' (2.1.5) while John himself remained onstage as a frozen subject, and then left as Beatrice continued by comparing John to Benedick. While the comparison theoretically notes their differences, what resonated most was their similarity.

Benedick's isolation was emphasized further by the unusual closeness of Pedro and Claudio. Dominic Cavendish identified the soldiers' first appearance as displaying 'absurd, latently homosexual horseplay' (1998), but Cheek by Jowl pushed this from horseplay into a clear set of emotional stakes for these two characters. When Pedro announced that he had wooed Hero for Claudio (2.1.274), Hero (Sarita Choudhary) stepped forward towards Claudio. Claudio, who had walked into the auditorium in anger at Pedro, paused, then returned to the stage, marched straight past Hero and embraced Pedro, leaving Hero alone and mortified. Brian Logan identifies this as 'one of Donnellan's several comic coups' (1998), indicative of Claudio preferring his cohort to a woman. As Kamaralli notes, however, it also 'drew attention to the character's lack of lines in this scene' (2012: 114), emphasized further as Claudio then shook Leonato's hand before finally, awkwardly, turning to Hero. Claudio and Pedro continued to be drawn together – as Pedro announced his plan to bring Beatrice and Benedick together (2.1.339), he and Claudio stood with arms around one another while Hero stood patiently to the side of the happy pair. The two's closeness became more obnoxious as they bullied Benedick in 3.2. Benedick hid a bunch of flowers behind his back as they teased him, tore the flowers from his hand and threw them up in the air. As Benedick left with Leonato, Claudio and Pedro whooped and made noises of mock offence at his retreating back, holding onto one another as they laughed. Then, left alone, they fell quiet, looked at one another and started drawing closer together; Don John's arrival interrupted them before they could kiss.

Donnellan describes his changing attitudes towards *Much Ado about Nothing* as he directed it:

> the more you actually start to really pay *Much Ado* the respect of finding out what is happening in it the more appalling the play seems to become ... I thought I was starting to loathe the play ... I hated what it seemed to imply about that relationship of two men [Don Pedro and Claudio] using an unsuspecting woman [Hero] to stabilize themselves. The more you start to look at it the more you realize there's just something very unpleasant in the play. But then we are not there just to put on nice things. Sometimes we need to look at what we hate, or what frightens us or what makes us feel uncomfortable. And to try to look at that unflinchingly, and without judging. (Donnellan 2018)[5]

Donnellan's distaste for what the company's process revealed to him about the play is significant. A Cheek by Jowl production does not create the world he and Ormerod want to see, but a world that offers the most alive reflection of an empathetic exploration of the text. 'I don't "see" the play in my head before I enter the rehearsal room, or indeed during the rehearsal process, and I may not like what I have done when the performance goes on' (Donnellan 1999: 20). This ethos allowed the company to confront head-on the problems at the heart of the play, looking unflinchingly at the connection between Pedro and Claudio that led to their use and abuse of Hero. Claire McEachern notes that one of the most important decisions a production now has to make is 'how ruthlessly "patriarchal" a world emerges in production, in which patriarchy is principally understood as a system of male alliance and rivalry conducted through the exchange of and competition for women' (2016: 85). The production's distaste culminated in the wedding scene.

The wedding scene was foreshadowed by the overlapping transitions of the scenes that led up to it, which set up opposing sides. At the conclusion of 3.4, when the arrival of the men was announced, Pedro, Claudio, Benedick and Don John appeared upstage, speaking their own names and standing in an intimidating line while the women stood downstage. With the men in full military uniform and Hero only partially dressed, the visual imbalance established the tone that would lead to her orchestrated shaming. The men remained in their upstage line throughout Leonato's interview with Dogberry and Verges (3.5), the projected subjects beautifully tying together the plot strands by making visible the men who were both instigators and victims of Borachio and Conrade's plot.

This led directly into a wedding scene (4.1), which began with men and women separated on either side singing a hymn, before Leonato walked the veiled Hero slowly downstage. The formal separation of the sexes established the spatial terms for Claudio's coldly formal rejection. He kept a distance from Hero, before performing a mock marriage by leading her over to Leonato and joining their hands. He then walked offstage into the auditorium, distancing himself as far as possible from Hero as he shouted his accusations against her chastity. The effect of this was to lend his words the quality of a voice-over, with everyone on stage more or less frozen as Claudio's vocalization of her guilt resounded – for a moment, they all became his projected subjects, and by standing amid the audience he forcibly aligned their perspective with his own, insisting they see Hero as he did. Pedro offered icy support with his cold 'I stand dishonoured' (4.1.63), contrasting with the heat of Benedick's outrage at the accusations. The accusers' performance was designed to disrupt any of Hero's attempts at defence. She took a Bible to swear on, which Pedro snatched from her hand. Throughout, Hero remained dignified; it was only when Leonato collapsed, beaten, into Claudio's arms on 'Has no man's dagger a point for me?' (4.1.109) that Hero also fell. On the departure of the accusers, the stage space was re-orientated around Hero's fallen body. The women gathered closely around her, while Leonato stayed at the edges of the stage to shout his anger. Benedick stood between Leonato and the women, moving with Leonato to continually position himself as a protective barrier for the women. The instinctive and generous defensive act epitomized Benedick's liminal position at this point, neither part of the group of women nor one of the attackers, and his separation from both cast him as a man alone.

Benedick's isolation was mirrored throughout by Beatrice's. The *New York Times* review is revealing of its own values when it describes her as 'a brittle bluestocking ... finding Freudian anxiety beneath the flinty bravado of a self-declared new woman' (Brantley 1998). To judge a woman in such loaded terms for keeping her distance amid a society that valorized such toxic, braying masculinity is perhaps to miss the point. Beatrice refused to make herself vulnerable to the same kind of victimization that Hero was subject to, and regularly kept herself at the sides of the stage and/or at some distance from those she talked to; when she did get close to others, it was often in positions of control, such as leading Hero in a dance, or putting her foot on Hero's back as she pulled the laces of her corset tight; an image Robert Smallwood describes as 'the female body being prepared to come to the altar and to her man – like trussing up a chicken for consumption' (1999: 234). When she and Benedick sniped at one another during the ball (2.1.113–40), they withdrew to the downstage corners to lean against the proscenium arch, keeping as much distance between each other – and the rest of the party – as possible.

Beatrice's merriment was defensive, but not bravado. Her sadness was no posture but deeply rooted, as evident during her delivery of 'My mother cried; but then there was a star danced, and under that was I born' (2.1.308–10). Brantley read this as 'an unsettled anger that bespeaks infinite fear of sex and childbirth', a reading for which I saw no justification; Beatrice was desperately sad, stepping away from Pedro and speaking soberly, hinting at a mother who had not survived childbirth; Reeves 'never settled on just one story ... I would imagine she died while giving birth ... or I would imagine that her mother had never wanted a girl' (2003: 31). Beatrice 'proceeded to get drunk to the point of falling over, as an expression of resentment of the whole milieu', adding a comic note to the complex sadness underpinning Reeves's performance (Kamaralli 2012: 116). Beatrice actively kept herself at a distance from emotional connection, her isolation matching Benedick's, generated by his uptight fussiness and inability to participate in the general domestic setting. The two poured this isolation into their verbal sparring. As Donnellan puts it,

> Beatrice and Benedick, of course, use their wit to hide their feelings. I think one of the most foolish ways of looking at Beatrice and Benedick is that you direct them as if they are witty, sophisticated people. They'd *like* to be witty, sophisticated people, they would *prefer* to be witty, sophisticated people ... we can use our articulacy to separate ourselves from each other, just as we can even use sex to be less intimate with somebody: we can actually use words to deny communication with other people. (2003: 163)

The readings of these two characters led to relatively sober interpretations of the two overhearing scenes. Act 2, scene 2 played as a transitional scene, in which the four conspirators in the plot to make Beatrice and Benedick fall in love – Margaret, Hero, Pedro and Claudio – remained onstage as frozen subjects at the end of 2.1. As Borachio explained his plot to Don John, he spun these four figures around, demonstrating his control of them, as if they were no more than four plates he was keeping in motion. Benedick walked through these four as he arrived for 2.3, underscoring his twinned isolation from both the friends who were planning to gull him and the more malign conspiracy. The overhearing began with a pratfall – in the recorded performance, Benedick lay on the ledge of one of the theatre's side boxes and fell into it while flailing at the mention of Beatrice's love for him.

But the remainder of the scene was played with sincerity, Benedick listening intently to the others, especially as they placed emphasis on Beatrice's danger (2.3.170). Left alone, he delivered his soliloquy in two quiet, sober parts. After 'I will be horribly in love with her' (226–7), he walked slowly upstage, but then paused, held his head, then braced himself against an onstage bench. Steeling himself, he delivered the remainder of the speech with a forcefulness approaching anger, building up to his cry of 'The world must be peopled' (233). 'It was only when Benedict burst into tears as the truth of Beatrice's love finally hit him that masculinity appeared able to break through the mask of stultifying child's play and take on women face to face,' suggests Carol Rutter (2005: 349). The force of emotion stressed this as a major turning point; as Macfadyen says, 'I remember in rehearsal having the idea of laughing and the laughter turning into weeping with the joy of it, with the newness of it' (2016).

Act 2, scene 3 was thus not a mere comic set piece but a critical point in Benedick's development. McEachern argues that the 'gulling of Benedick, for instance, works by flattering him, whereas Beatrice's gullers undertake a kind of scourging of her faults' (2016: 64); in Cheek by Jowl's version, however, the emphasis was on Benedick learning empathy for someone whose feelings he had hitherto not acknowledged. Kamaralli notes that the gulling 'has the unintended side-effect of causing him to reject [homosocial] priorities and align himself with the women' (2012: 115–16), as revealed in the defensive posture he took during the wedding. Reeves's performance during the overhearing scene similarly emphasized the emotional significance of her 'discovery', as she sneaked downstage to hide behind Ursula and Hero. As with Benedick's scene, there was almost no physical comedy – simply Beatrice, silent and listening. Following her reflective line 'Stand I condemned for pride and scorn so much?' (3.1.108), she paused for a long time before answering her question in a firm, kindly tone, emphasizing the 'kindness' in 'my kindness shall incite thee' (113). Beatrice, like Benedick, 'listens, probably for the first time' (Reeves 2003: 38), and resolved to try to understand the other.

Left alone at the end of 4.1, Beatrice and Benedick stood at opposite sides of the stage, shell-shocked. Hero's situation informed their interactions across the play's second half. Here, they spoke slowly, seriously, with little tone or inflection as they confessed their love for one another, sadly and simply in the light of what had just happened. But having exposed themselves and learned empathy, they took their time as they each escalated what they were asking of the other. Beatrice paused for a long time before asking Benedick to 'Kill Claudio' (4.1.288), 'a pause in which fury was barely contained and which left not the faintest possibility of laughter in the house' (Smallwood 1999: 234). Benedick similarly delayed before saying, 'Not ... for the wide world' (289). Beatrice responded by reverting to formality, walking over and shaking his hand. But, as she tried to leave, he grabbed her wrist, preventing her from leaving. In disrupting her act of poised departure in a show of control, Benedick incited her to anger – she erupted and moved about the stage, shouting at him as he stood stock still. Only as she tried to leave again after 'I will die a woman with grieving' (321) did he finally betray his own emotion, shouting 'Tarry' (322). Mirroring her behaviours, he became formal, announcing, 'I am engaged' (328), before walking over, kissing her hand and turning to leave; as he had done to her, she now grabbed his hand to stop him leaving. The scene closed with them holding hands as he agreed to fight on her behalf, indicating the elision of the space that had hitherto separated them.

As the Beatrice and Benedick plot resolved, the production repeated two sets of motifs from earlier scenes, leading Logan to note 'the extent to which, in a reversal of the axiom, *Much Ado* repeats as tragedy in its second half what it introduces as farce in its first' (1998). In 5.1, as Benedick challenged Claudio, they restaged the earlier teasing of 3.2. This time, Benedick held a gage behind his back instead of flowers; this time, he revealed what he was hiding on his own terms, addressing

Claudio formally and presenting him with the gage. Pedro's attempts to tease Benedick with comments about Beatrice were now more overtly cruel; Beatrice appeared as a projected figure as he spoke, walking around Benedick as Pedro described her comments (5.1.156–68). Benedick reached out to the projection as she left the stage, and as she disappeared he exploded in rage at Claudio's 'the married man' (179), taking Pedro and Claudio aback. Reining in his anger, he kneeled before Pedro and made a formal request to leave his service. This done, the meeting between Beatrice and Benedick in 5.2 then reprised their leave-taking at the end of 4.1. On 'Only foul words – and thereupon I will kiss thee (5.2.47–8), Benedick walked to Beatrice and bent his head to kiss her, but she began speaking as their lips almost touched, preventing the kiss. A few lines later, the position was reversed – after 'subscribe him a coward' (55), Beatrice leaned up to kiss him, and he prevented it with 'Now tell me' (56). Benedick finally acknowledge that 'Thou and I are too wise to woo peaceably' (67), and strode across the stage for a third attempt at a kiss, interrupted by the shout of the discovery of the plot. Benedick, thwarted, resorted to formality, kneeling to declare his faith to Beatrice.

The final two scenes reintegrated the community, with a notable exception. Hero appeared upstage during 5.3 as the lament was sung, and took charge of unveiling herself directly in front of Claudio in the final scene. Where earlier it had been Benedick who laughed inappropriately at Claudio's love for Hero, in a fitting reversal it was now Don Pedro who laughed loudly, quickly stopping when he realized he was alone. Claudio threw himself at Hero's feet, and she stepped away briefly before allowing him to take her hand and embrace her. As they embraced, the whole ensemble came together to lay their hands on the pair, with the exception of Pedro, who stood conspicuously off to the side. With Claudio and Hero reconciled, the production allowed for a moment of comedy as Beatrice and Benedick chased about the stage to get hold of the letters they had written (Beatrice ate hers), but on 'Peace! I will stop your mouth' (5.4.97), Benedick took Beatrice's face firmly in his hands and finally kissed her. Everyone stood in absolute silence, marking the moment's importance, until they parted.

Empathy led to the reforming of bonds, as visualized in the laying on and holding of hands between all parties. Claudio held out a hand to Benedick, but Benedick embraced him instead. Beatrice initially refused Claudio's hand, but eventually agreed to shake it; David Nathan noted that the 'quality of Declan Donnellan's directorial insight can be gauged by his use of one of Benedick's final lines, "Come, come, we are friends," not as a general goodwill platitude', but in the cause of bringing the community back together (1998). All of the contact drew attention to Pedro's continued isolation, stressed in the now-common emphasis on the line 'Prince, thou art sad' (5.4.120). While the production didn't offer a moral judgement, it was clear that Mangan's Pedro remained at the play's conclusion one of the few who had not sufficiently learned empathy, and the unity of the conclusion was undermined by a final use of a projected figure. Don John returned to the stage, and the two brothers reached out for one another – but were prevented by the reunited couples walking between them as they began a closing dance, keeping them separate. The close alignment of empathy and physical contact, and Pedro's isolation from both, made for a reflective final point in a production that insisted that any joy had to be earned.

Measure for Measure

It is increasingly rare for any joy to be found in productions of *Measure for Measure*, a play whose insistence on balance means that all gains and losses are qualified. Kenji Yoshino suggests, from a legal perspective, that the play argues for a *via media*, demonstrating 'that no sane person would wish to live in a world governed either solely by empathy, or solely by the letter of the law' (2009: 684). This balance, of course, depends on characters actually *achieving* some kind of empathetic consideration for one another's predicaments, making it a rich study for Cheek by Jowl. The company first produced the play in English in 1994, a production in which 'the Duke and Angelo are doppelgangers, both control freaks, both, in their different ways, angling to get their hands on Isabella'; the Duke literally so 'actively manhandling the play's personnel into tableaux of his choice as though they were so many shop dummies' (Taylor 1994). In returning to the play almost twenty years later, the company explored further how a play so concerned with manipulation (legal and physical) can engage empathetic connections.

Penny Gay notes that the main late twentieth-century trends in the play offered 'various attempts to explain – to allegorise or humanise – the character of the Duke; to engage some sympathy for Angelo ... and, in Isabella, to examine the possibilities for female power in an entrenched patriarchy' (1994: 121). In Cheek by Jowl's production, this was partly realized by bolstering the presence of two figures – Claudio and Barnardine – as projected subjects central to the play's emotional stakes.[6] Isabella, Angelo and the Duke all, to some extent, act in their own interests while purporting to represent the general good; the visible presence of victims such as Claudio and Barnardine – as well as the near-constant presence of the whole ensemble – kept clear the fact that their actions had consequences for a wider community (Kirwan 2018: 164). I will return to these important figures later.

In the opening moments of the production, described in this book's Introduction, the Duke's (Alexander Arsentyev) isolation was established by separating him from the ensemble.[7] The Duke was troubled, practically pleading with Escalus (Iurii Rumiantcev) for understanding, and in 1.3 kneeling before the Friar to demand his blessing. His desperation to be understood, even while refusing to reveal his true intentions, indicated the contradictions implicit in a character defined by both apparent insecurity and extreme overconfidence. An overlapping transition between 1.3 and 2.1 juxtaposed his lines 'Lord Angelo is precise; Stands at a guard with envy;

Scarce confesses / That his blood flows' (1.3.50–2) with an image of the ensemble raising Angelo (Andrei Kuzichev) bodily into a light as a paragon of virtue; the Duke was apparently unaware of the irony as this holy Angelo spoke, 'We must not make a scarecrow of the law' (2.1.1). With the Duke and Angelo set up visually as doppelgangers of one another, the production repeatedly underlined the easy slippage between two figures acting in the name of their society, but ultimately for themselves.

Anna Khalilulina's Isabella was central to the play, the focus of the Duke and Angelo's power plays, and herself the driving protagonist of the play's most emotional scenes. The central battle between Isabella and Angelo, played out across 2.2 and 2.4, saw two people forced to engage with one another without any initial desire to understand or empathize. At the start of 2.2, Isabella stood, angry and firm, distant from Angelo, who sat behind a desk writing and ignoring her. Lucio (Alexander Feklistov) urged Isabella to draw closer to him, but her body was angled away. It was only as he dismissed her that she leaned in more forcefully, resistant to being told what to do, and as both Lucio and Angelo gave her orders, she asserted her independence more strongly. But it was a different tactic that finally made Angelo pay attention: Isabella went downstage, knelt and began praying. Angelo, moved into a show of piety, came and joined her to offer his prayers, but then returned to his desk. It was in eventual frustration at his lack of empathy – or even interest – that she lunged over his desk, clutched at his jacket and shook him out of his quiet, finally ruffling him. As Lucio led her away, sobbing, Angelo opened up Claudio's file and said, 'I will bethink me' (2.2.145). Isabella ran back to kneel before him and kiss his hand. Her gestural language became imploring and grateful, she facing him straight on, opening up her arms in a performance of thanks.

The dynamic was reversed after her departure, though. Left alone at the end of 2.2, Angelo stood in a spotlight and allowed his formal facade to unravel, energetically pacing as he became aroused and unsettled. He knelt down next to the chair in which Isabella had sat, feeling its warmth before sniffing and rubbing his face in it. As he did this, the rest of the ensemble moved across, silently standing in judgement. The sequence established the repressed tendencies hitherto only hinted at; 2.4 made them explicit, following directly on from 2.2 so that Angelo began the second interview in the same slightly dishevelled state. He took a few moments to establish his public face, putting on his glasses and adjusting his lapel handkerchief before resuming his seat. It didn't take long, however, for this performance to unravel. He stood up and took off his suit jacket, exposing himself as Isabella became angry at Angelo's evasive answers, and raised his voice to match hers. Then, on his admission that 'I love you' (2.4.140), her eyes widened in shock, she unable to believe what she was hearing. She turned her back on him in disdain, before turning back again with laughter on her face as she promised to proclaim him (150), and she confidently pushed the release forms towards him. The direct threat prompted an aggressive defence from Angelo. He gestured towards the theatre audience, asking, 'Who will believe thee?' (153), a moment Pascale Aebischer describes as 'a rhetorical question … secure in his interpretation of the audience as deeply compromised by their silent acquiescence to his corruption' (Aebischer, forthcoming). In this security, he took off his glasses, unbuckled his belt, then pushed her back onto the table and knelt down before her, pulling up her skirts and shushing her, removing her shoe and kissing her feet 'like a famished animal' (Cavendish 2015a). She pulled away, and he responded by pinning her down and clawing at her clothes; the watching ensemble suddenly burst into life, rushing over as she bit him, and forced him to withdraw. Angelo remained onstage, writing, as Isabella appealed to the same audience with whom Angelo had assumed complicity.

The abuse of power, and easy assumption of invulnerability by a man in power, established a message read by some critics as political; Maxim Boon noted that 'In the era of "grab 'em by the pussy" via the hypocrisy of alt-righteous moralising and petulant tweets, it is horribly believable that authoritarians are capable of using their power to target individuals. Isabella's refusal to submit no longer stands as an act of piety, but rather a political protest' (2017). The production's condemnation of Angelo (and by extension any number of abusers in political power) was well taken. But in the scene that followed, a more complex set of implications was teased out in relation to her own empathy for her brother. Khalilulina notes that Isabella 'has a goal and it is a very clear one for her – she is determined to save her brother. So the scene with Claudio is the key one for Isabella' (2017). Claudio has little stage time in *Measure for Measure*, yet he is the focus of Isabella's attention, and the double-sided stakes – 'I will save Claudio / I will not save Claudio' – are some of the highest and clearest in Shakespeare. Yet 3.1 is the scene in which she tells Claudio that he will need to die, as she cannot do what is required to save him.

Isabella's need for Claudio (Petr Rykov) was trailed earlier, he appearing as a projected subject to whom she reached out as Lucio spoke of him in 1.4. When they finally met in person, they began on either side of a table, recalling her interviews with Angelo. The contrast was in Claudio's energy; he banged the table, impatient for news, then was overcome by emotion, falling to his knees and pummelling the air. Isabella took him in her arms and held him in her lap as he sobbed in fear. But it was while they were in this position that she revealed the condition she would not fulfil. He initially laughed, thinking he was saved, then affirmed that she would not do it. But as she soothed him with the words of Psalm 23, he began reflecting on what death would be like and became agitated. He took his shirt off, forcing Isabella's hands onto his chest, asking her to recognize his embodied experience of his suffering. She stood up, leaving him kneeling before her, and after a long pause he asked, quietly and firmly, 'let me live' (3.1.132). She reacted in rage, slapping him down; he responded, shockingly, by overpowering her and, just as Angelo had done, lifting her skirts and pawing at her. Noah Birksted-Breen, a rare reviewer who commented on this moment, suggests the inspiration was taken from Isabella's line 'It's not a kind of incest, to take life / From thine own sister's shame?' (138–9), noting that it showed 'a moral weakness ... extended into an act of physical aggression' (2016: 89). Attempting to take control of his sister's body in a desperate attempt to save himself, the extremity of the stakes for Claudio – death/life – drove the production to breaking point, beginning the bravura sequence depicted on the cover of this book.

A double bass was brought out, and Claudio ran his hands over it as if a female body, shouting the displaced lines 'If I must die / I will encounter darkness as a bride' (82–3). He then began plucking out a waltz on the bass, channelling the assault on Isabella into the force with which he tore at the notes. Centre stage, playing the bass as if his life depended on it, a dance of death began around him, the Duke leading the ensemble in a mimicry of *The Seventh Seal*. A recorded waltz soundtrack joined the notes of the bass, and the Duke took Isabella's hand at the start of a human chain as he explained the bed trick. Projected subjects emerged to present Mariana (Elmira Mirel) drinking and Angelo presenting her with a ring. Isabella was deposited with Mariana, then the grinning Angelo, whom she blindfolded. He held out his hand in expectation, until Mariana, clapping her hands, summoned him to her. Angelo and Mariana waltzed centre stage as the human chain encircled them; the two danced out of sight, and the rest of the ensemble span around Claudio, still spotlit. Then the recorded music stopped, and 4.2 resumed in the prison while Claudio continued violently plucking at the bass, the slapping disrupting the melody as Angelo's letter arrived. As the Provost finished reading the letter (4.2.118–24), Claudio suddenly stopped playing. He picked up the bass, walked towards the audience, and then off upstage, as the Duke lunged towards him and missed. This sequence, which only emerged in the final days of rehearsal (Donnellan and Ormerod 2016), threaded together 3.1–4.2 in a five-minute sequence centred on Claudio's body, he becoming the source of all of the sequence's action.

By visually and aurally placing Claudio at the heart of the production, Cheek by Jowl refused to allow the Duke or Isabella any easy solutions. Claudio's 'death' was another turning point for Isabella. When she learned of it (4.3.115), the Duke and Angelo were set up in opposing spotlights, Angelo at his desk with a bloodied head in a bag before him. As the Duke spoke, in a typical moment of Cheek by Jowl spatial fluidity, Isabella crossed between the two lit areas, reached out and touched her brother's head, living out the projected image. She cried out, collapsed to the floor and let out an unholy scream. However justified her choices had been, the production forced her to confront their consequences.

The Duke, by contrast, was positioned against a different figure to face the consequences of his lack of empathy. From the production's first entrance into the prison in 2.3, the Duke had been haunted by a figure in convict uniform (Igor Teplov). This tall, dishevelled man was regularly at the front of the watching ensemble but remained unidentified. At the Duke's lowest point, however, the man came to the fore as Barnardine. From a flurry of ensemble movement, during which Barnardine's story was heard shouted out, a pool of light suddenly revealed Barnardine, half-naked, lying on the Duke's lap like a child – or like the body of Christ in Mary's arms. Barnardine pleaded with the Duke and kissed his face, and the waltz music began again. Barnardine pulled the Duke to his feet, and led him in a macabre reprisal of the dance of death – only now it was the two of them alone. The set – a series of red cubes against a black backdrop – jumped into life, with three of the cubes beginning to rotate, revealing contained within them the images of Claudio strapped to an electric chair; Isabella frozen like a music box doll; and Pompey shagging a prostitute. Barnardine, gaining an infernal confidence that resisted control, spun the Duke around, throwing him to the floor and leaving him crawling in a nightmarish world of his own failings. As Stephen Purcell suggests, 'The production seemed to be staging a confrontation between the Duke and his sublimated thoughts about death, desire and sexuality' (2016: 402). The Duke's discovery of what it meant to face death – and to be unprepared for it – became his own moment of revelation. As Angelo and Escalus prepared for the Duke's return (4.4), the Duke rejoined the watching ensemble and Barnardine embraced the Duke protectively from behind, indicating the impact of the encounter on him. The Duke's close encounter with death enacted a powerful hold on him that informed the production's resolution.

This resolution took on a more overtly political edge. A red carpet was rolled out and a microphone placed while the Duke re-dressed himself in his suit in full view of the audience; a reminder of the performative nature of his return. Aebischer observes that 'Canned cheers greeted his arrival as he approached the downstage centre microphone to address the audience like a totalitarian leader with a personality cult' (forthcoming; see Figure 6). Birksted-Breen notes that UK reviewers repeatedly made connections to Putin, although these were not reflected in the Russian reviews; while the comparison was perhaps inevitable, the critique of power politics here was hardly applicable to any single ruler (2016: 89–90). The scene moved the action into the public sphere, with the Duke bellowing his pronouncements into the microphone while Escalus and Angelo flanked him, the Duke's performance of confidence contrasting markedly with his recent nervous encounter with Barnardine.

The use of the microphone established the disparity of the power structure, with Isabella and later Mariana shouting their complaints unamplified from the back of the auditorium while the Duke responded through the microphone. Isabella was invited to speak into the microphone, but Angelo quickly grabbed it back from her while uniformed officers wrangled her away, one placing his hand over her mouth. The Duke's performance of authority was also a performance of a state machinery that denied empathy, or even competing voices, and it put Isabella through further physical and emotional trauma. Her experience was repeated with Mariana, who was similarly quickly taken away from the microphone. The repeated sight of women being silenced, followed by the Duke giving Angelo right of reply into the microphone, sent out a chilling message

FIGURE 6 *Escalus (Iurii Rumiantcev), the Duke (Alexander Arsentyev) and Angelo (Andrei Kuzichev). Photograph by Johan Persson/ArenaPAL; www.arenapal.com.*

about state-approved views, in an echo of Boon's comments. Angelo's announcement that the women were set on by some higher power resonated with contemporaneous claims of conspiracy levelled against victims of sexual assault, and the women were repeatedly sidelined until the Duke could complete his carefully stage-managed performance of his own magnificence. As William Drew suggests, 'The man with real power gets away with everything' (2015).

Yet the production didn't let the Duke off the hook. His revelation from under the Friar's cowl was greeted with complete silence, and his first act in his revelation was to order the police to manhandle Lucio away. His dictates were played with some humour – an ecstatic Mariana kissed Angelo hard on the lips before dragging him off. But his 'reunion' with Isabella showed his inability to suddenly shrug off the power imbalance; even though he now addressed her without amplification and softened his voice, he was inseparable from the public figure who turned back to the microphone to announce Angelo's death sentence. This continued ambivalence made Isabella's act – as she stepped forward, lowered herself to the floor and quietly, not without conflict, asked for Angelo's life – all the more transcendent. The transformation from her uncontrollable scream that she would 'pluck out his eyes!' (5.3.119) was absolute and, perhaps – in keeping with her earlier obstinacy in 2.2 – a direct response to the Duke's revelation of his own manipulation.

The Duke's own reckoning came as Barnardine was brought out, a bag over his head. Three officers forced him to the floor, where he sat looking up in fear at everyone. The confident Duke waved his security aside and knelt to take Barnardine's hand, but Barnardine leaped at him. The guards jumped in and drew their weapons, leaving Barnardine screaming in a foetal position. Again the Duke approached, and gently removed Barnardine's restraints; the prisoner got up, slowly, and then ran from the stage. The departure of the Duke's familiar left a sour taste; the Duke had clearly expected gratitude or a connection, and instead found he had squandered any empathy for the sake of public display. The subsequent unveiling of Claudio was similarly intended to be a triumphant coup, and the Duke held out his arms as if expecting applause. Isabella, however, looked aghast at the betrayal while simultaneously overjoyed to see her brother. She walked towards Claudio and kneeled in supplication, aiming to embrace his legs, but he stepped around her and walked away; reminiscent, perhaps, of the 1994 production in which 'Saved, but not by his sister, Claudio pushed Isabella roughly away' (Rutter 2005: 348). Isabella tore off her headscarf, finally revealing her hair and rejecting her earlier vocation, while Claudio instead went over to Juliet (Anastasia Lebedeva), who was holding their baby. The Duke took the opportunity to ask for Isabella's hand, but she walked past him and watched, excluded, while her brother embraced his family.

Measure for Measure, not dissimilarly to *Much Ado about Nothing*, concluded with an ambiguously happy ending, marked by a display of joy from which some were excluded. The Duke covered his embarrassment at being ignored by shouting to the audience, celebrating his triumph and punishing Lucio, before turning back to Isabella, who again ignored him. As the sounds of the waltz started up again, the production closed on three sharply contrasting dances. Claudio and Juliet danced closely together, inseparable. Mariana dragged Angelo out and led him, he limp as a doll in her arms. And finally, sadly, Isabella allowed the Duke to take her hand, she first, however, grabbing her headscarf back from him. With the three pairs clearly separate from one another, and some dancers barely able to look at their partners, the unity of the dance sharply underlined the loneliness that remained.

Conclusions

I think we're not born with empathy. I also think we're not born able to love. I think we are born with the capacity to develop these functions. That is all. What we are born with, already in place, is a ferocious sense of attachment. But this is not love. We can't possibly love someone until we can see them, which is the same moment that we realise they are different from us. That takes some time and some experience. Without these we can have attachment, we can have passion, but we can't call it love. Just as there's a difference between concentration and attention, there is also a huge distance between sympathy and empathy ... And we make terrible mistakes with too much sympathy, and too little empathy. (Donnellan 2018)[8]

Donnellan's views on empathy, on the importance of attempting to understand things that you cannot feel yourself, led to explorations that held the characters of *Much Ado about Nothing* and *Measure for Measure* uncompromisingly to account for their actions and choices. The company's productions do not lend themselves to simplistic moral frameworks but, rather, explore the implications of what happens when characters respond in the living moment to 'predicaments', to use a word that has become more important in Donnellan's recent thinking (Donnellan 2018).[9] This is paralleled in the theory underpinning the process, a direct consequence of an acting company taking an externalized approach, in which the aim is not to understand yourself but to respond to what is happening in the space. As ever, Donnellan puts it most clearly in *The Actor and the Target*:

We can either show or see, but we can never do both, for the one must destroy the other ... Seeing is about the target, showing is about me. Showing only seems to be about the target. Showing is in fact a false opening of oneself, because showing is about trying to control the perception of others. (2005: 80)

Donnellan's advice about responding to the external can be read as a call for empathy in practice. The Duke's self-presentation in the final scene of *Measure for Measure* was perhaps the most explicit manifestation of a character showing, not seeing; his focus on himself prevented him from developing empathy for Isabella, resulting in her continued isolation and only reluctant taking of his hand at that production's conclusion. Conversely, Beatrice and Benedick's attempts to acknowledge each other's experience and needs, while imperfect, allowed them an ending denied to Don Pedro and Don John. The objectified bodies of Hero, Claudio and Barnardine, meanwhile, uncompromisingly displayed onstage to make clear the impacts of selfish actions, ensured that the serious stakes at the hearts of these comedies remained central to the ensemble's choices. The clearly visible loneliness of several of the comedies' characters at the ends of both productions, following the emotional logic and textual clues of the plays themselves, offered an effective counter to the figures of authority who insisted that all was well.

The unity of Cheek by Jowl's productions, honed over thirty-seven years by a consistent creative team and developed with an ensemble ethos, makes the singling out of individual contributions to any one production both impossible and meaningless. The philosophical, conceptual and performative integrity of a Cheek by Jowl production is dependent on empathy, on recognizing that the individual does not have all answers and emotions within themselves, and thus cannot ever be self-reliant. The aliveness of a Cheek by Jowl production comes from avoiding the 'false openings' of self-aggrandizing display or attempts to control perception, and from striving towards an understanding and acknowledgement of one another. The end results may not be happy, but they will be alive.

Conclusion: evolutions

Cheek by Jowl's work is in a state of constant evolution. This is manifest at all levels – in the projects and collaborations that Donnellan and Ormerod seek out; in the shifts that each production makes over the course of its run; and in the nightly variations inevitable when a company is living in the space rather than working to repeat fixed points. A production never settles – Donnellan suggests that he (and Ormerod) 'go once a week to see Cheek by Jowl productions' on average (1999: 21), a figure that the archives suggest may well be conservative. Matthew Macfadyen remembers that 'We'd be in Cheltenham or Bogota or somewhere, and he had the notes sessions, which were searingly funny and brilliant and terrifying – but we would not stop working on the play. We'd have, like, three shows left, and he gave us notes, after a hundred-odd shows and ten months of touring' (2016). The extraordinary investment in the tour and in the production marks Donnellan and Ormerod out as near-unique – where other directors might leave the tour to their assistant directors and go on to the next job, Cheek by Jowl's artistic team remain present.

> They are the people most committed to touring. And they actually like it. I've seen them with their mini-bar in Prague, you know ... They like being in hotels, they like travelling; they love new environments, they are very good in public relations, they like new theatres. They are genuinely excited by it. They're

not boring sit-at-homes. They do want to get out there and learn and see and do it. (Michael Coveney in Reade 1991: 19)

The desire to explore the unknown rather than settle for what the company already knows about itself is connected to Donnellan's interest in empathy, as discussed in the previous chapter. The restless desire to explore each new situation, each new venue and audience, each new reading – even if it emerges right at the end of a run – is key to the company's ongoing vitality. 'For us,' Donnellan suggested in 1989, 'the central moment of theatre is when the audience's imagination and the actors' imagination are perfectly joined, and something is born between them' (Berry 1989: 202). This shared experience, refreshed nightly, leads to constant renewal.

Some evolutions in a production are more noticeable than others. When *The Winter's Tale* first premiered in Sceaux in January 2016, the scene between Autolycus, the Old Shepherd and the Clown that concludes 4.4 (687–847) was a heavily rewritten comic set piece. Autolycus (Ryan Donaldson) posed as a border control guard – stealing money, going through their bags, performing an impromptu cavity search on the shocked Clown (Sam McArdle). What was an amusing scene with invasive undertones, however, evolved into something much more troubling. During the hiatus between the production's initial European tour (January–March 2016) and revival (December 2016–June 2017), 37 per cent of the UK electorate voted to leave the European Union, prompting the government to enact Brexit. For a company that creates and tours work across Europe and has a model and reputation built on international touring, the decision was disastrous.

When the production reached London in April 2017, the airport scene had changed markedly. Now, Autolycus subjected the Shepherds to a long list of security questions – 'hast thou packed thy fardel thyself?' – and requested disease clearance forms, parents' birth certificates, astrological charts, completed and countersigned ZDRX RPRZ 32, 33 and 34 and swearings of the Sicilian oath. The ludicrous parody of increased airport security was funny, all laughing in relief until the Clown realized he didn't have his 'P27'. In response, Autolycus took the Clown upstage and, in a moment that felt like a bucket of iced water over the audience when I saw it live, Autolycus proceeded to smack the Clown over the head, knocking him to the floor and stamping on him repeatedly before returning him, bloodied and dazed, to his father. The live stream on 10 April captured the impact beautifully, framing Peter Moreton's Shepherd in close up, too terrified to move or look, while Autolycus beat the Clown in the background. The scene finished with the Shepherd hustling the Clown offstage, telling him in a hushed voice, 'We are blessed to have known this man.'

The resonances of the moment were entirely overlooked by the British press, with only *The Times* noting that Autolycus was funny 'until, that is, he turns nasty and beats an innocent traveller to a pulp' (Marlowe 2017). Pascale Aebischer, however, observes the commentary on 'the violation of individuals' rights and limits on freedom of movement in the Trump-era, post-Brexit, Anglo-American world' (2017: 724). British reviewers were seemingly oblivious to the different accents in play; a Northern Irishman (Donaldson) was policing the border that a Dublin man (McArdle) was trying to cross. In the context of Brexit, this dystopic depiction of a hard Irish border – long before the question finally became pressing in UK headlines – was chilling, the implied 'Welcome to Britain' hanging over the silence that followed the beating of the Irishman. The choice of London reviewers to avoid overt comment on this moment inadvertently reflected the capital's avoidance of the broader Irish question at a time of national disintegration.

It is rare that a Cheek by Jowl production has such explicit political resonance – but that is perhaps because such resonance is left to the interpreter. Alec Pattison of the British Council admitted that they had anticipated that the 1988–9 *Tempest* might resonate in Romania (see Chapter 4), expecting 'a clash between the traditional, government controlled art which they were used to, and the free and lively individualistic Cheek by Jowl' (Reade 1991: 85). Yet, upon seeing Anne White's Queen of Naples, compared to Margaret Thatcher in Britain, Simon Reade notes that the Romanian audience were in hysterics 'that White had managed to get their First Lady, Elena Ceaușescu, down to a tee'. As Reade notes, 'People in power cut the same figure ... in the eye of the beholder' (1991: 85). Indeed, paradoxically, one of the things that perhaps makes Cheek by Jowl a political company is precisely its avoidance of concepts that restrict interpretive potential and its insistence that actors are instead alive in the moment. Fausto Cabra suggests:

> To stay ALIVE onstage (and without lowering the stakes of exceptional characters and situations) is certainly the most difficult challenge today, but surely the only one that's really necessary. Donnellan and Ormerod are among the very few artists in the world (and not only within the boundaries of theatre) who understand that this is the only area of investigation that is really vital and politically revolutionary today. (2018)

The company's spare, contemporary aesthetic and its interest in the relations between individuals have allowed audiences on six continents to respond in unexpected and passionately different ways to the work.

Much of what distinguished the company in its earliest years is so endemic to British theatre practice now that it can be easy to forget Cheek by Jowl's pioneering role. When Michael Billington grudgingly admitted that 'I have no objection to [Daniel] Kramer's device of occasionally overlapping scenes' (2017) in a review of the Globe's 2017 production of *Romeo and Juliet*, he referred to a device that had defined Cheek by Jowl's transitions since the early 1980s. The all-male *As You Like It* and *Twelfth Night* (Chapter 3) initiated a new era of explorations of all-male Shakespeare, most notably in the work of Edward Hall's company Propeller and the Original Practices experiments in the early years of Shakespeare's Globe (Purcell 2017: 172–87). And in an era when alternatives are barely thinkable, it is important to remember that the company's casting of a black actor even as Othello in 1982 'was unusual enough to draw comment at the time' (Reade 1991: 65). Cheek by Jowl's commitment to casting non-white actors in principal roles led to the first performances on a British stage of characters such as Rosalind and Jaques by actors of colour, and the company's broader commitment to diverse casts (both in a company touring around the country and Europe and famously at the National Theatre for *Fuente Ovejuna*, 1989) was instrumental in helping normalize integrated casting (Rutter 2005: 346; Sierz 2010: 146). In 2018, when a critic can still ask if a black actor playing a classical character was 'cast because he is black?' and attribute the choice to 'politically correct casting' and a need 'to tick inclusiveness boxes' (Letts 2018), Cheek by Jowl's commitment to the right actor for the right role is as important a statement as ever.

It is, of course, fruitless to predict what Cheek by Jowl's next evolutions will be. Ormerod and Donnellan have been driving forward innovative practice for a year longer than this author has been alive, and in that time they have never stopped seeking new things, even if those new things are old, as in their influential revivals of European classics such as Racine's *Andromache* and Corneille's *The Cid* in the 1980s that Simon Reade celebrates as 'new, raw, and most importantly treated as such' (1991: 40). They retain the right, of course, to explore opportunities outside of the Cheek by Jowl structure, which have led to some of their most acclaimed, varied and visible work. Their legacy will be found in histories of new work (the London premiere of Tony Kushner's *Angels in America*, 1992–3), musical theatre (the world premiere of *Martin Guerre*, West End, 1996), ballet (*Romeo and Juliet* and *Hamlet* at the Bolshoi, 2004 and 2015) and opera (Verdi's *Falstaff* at the Salzburg Festival, 2001), and in 2012 they co-directed their first feature film, *Bel Ami*. But the two always return to Cheek by Jowl, the company and framework that allows them to produce the touring work based on their core principles, with the actor at the heart of the process.

In 2018, the company continues to innovate. As this book goes into production, the company has announced its first Russian production of a non-Shakespearean early modern play: Francis Beaumont's *The Knight of the Burning Pestle*, with long-time acting collaborators Alexander Feklistov, Anna Khalilulina, Andrei Kuzichev and Igor Teplov in the ensemble. Donnellan and Ormerod are also about to direct their first production with Italian actors, a version of Thomas Middleton's *The Revenger's Tragedy*. And the company is winning acclaim for its first Shakespeare production with the French company. Reuniting Xavier Boiffier, Christophe Grégoire, Cécile Leterme and Camille Cayol from *Andromaque* and *Ubu Roi*, *Périclès, Prince de Tyr* opened in Sceaux in March 2018, and at the time of writing is scheduled to tour France, the UK, Spain and Italy.

As with *'Tis Pity She's a Whore* and *Ubu Roi*, *Périclès* took place on a detailed set built around a single character – a patient in a psychiatric hospital (Grégoire). While the comatose patient's family were visiting him, the patient came to life as Périclès, and the play took over the bodies and objects that inhabit the ward: during his shipwreck, for instance, Périclès emptied a bedpan over himself, and the fishermen that rescued him were the doctor and nurses of the ward, patiently changing his bed and pyjamas and washing him down, before placing him into a straitjacket that served as the 'armour' for the jousting. The complex slippage between the world of the play and the world of the hospital ward, as with *Ubu*, cast the play as commentary on a more quotidian but deeply felt emotional situation – the present absence of the comatose patient from his family's lives, and the mutual desire for return. The production was not sentimental – the patient's seeming ambivalence about his daughter's partner (Boiffier) manifested in nightmarish visions as Périclès cast Boiffier repeatedly as the attempted assaulter of his daughter (Valentine Catzéflis): first as Antiochus and Antiochus's Daughter, then as Leonine, Lysimachus and Boult, who in turn attempted to kill, buy or rape Catzéflis's Marina.

The production epitomized two elements of Cheek by Jowl's current innovation that will serve as a fitting conclusion to the book. First is the production's radical interpretive doubling. *Périclès*, with a cast of only seven actors, involved all of the cast playing multiple roles, which were determined by broader thematic connections. Grégoire and Cayol – who played the patient's wife – recurrently became husband and wife: Périclès and Thaïsa; Cléon and Dionysa; Le Maître and La Maquerelle (Pander and Bawd). Meanwhile Leterme, the confident doctor in the hospital ward, became a series of carers: Simonide, bringing Périclès and Thaïsa together; Cérimon, bringing Thaïsa back to life; Diane, enacting a final reunion. The thoroughness of the doubling meant that each role carried resonances that transcended any individual 'character' – a term that Leterme, speaking of *Ubu*, felt was unhelpful for describing the kinds of role she takes on within a Cheek by Jowl production: 'I never thought of [my role] as a character. Of course she's a Queen, so she has to probably be in a certain way towards the audience and her husband and her son. But all these things are outside' (Leterme 2016). While doubling has always been a part of Cheek by Jowl's practice (Rutter 2005: 346; Prescott 2008: 77), *Périclès* made a feature of it that inverted the entire drama, exploring each character as a facet of a more important set of stakes: the longing for connection and reunion that drove the production to the final awakening of the patient.

At the other end of the scale – reception rather than production – *Périclès* marked the fourth time a Cheek by Jowl production had been broadcast live. Rather than the costly models favoured by institutional theatres such as the RSC or National Theatre, though, in which productions are broadcast into cinemas for paying audiences, Cheek by Jowl's broadcasts are free, high-quality web streams, going out live internationally and remaining available on the Cheek by Jowl website for a month (and often returning to the website), as I have discussed elsewhere (Kirwan 2018). Pascale Aebischer (forthcoming) talks about the creative affordance of Cheek by Jowl's web streams in extending the *platea* of a production's spatial organization, and the shift into allowing live streams acknowledges Donnellan and Ormerod's growing interest in film, both directing and its integration into theatrical *mise en scène*. Perhaps more importantly, though, it demonstrates Cheek by Jowl's commitment to its audiences. The costs of international touring mean that Cheek by Jowl cannot visit the sheer range of towns that marked its earliest tours, and even getting to a Cheek by Jowl production can thus become prohibitively expensive. The 'giving away' of its live streams allows the company to reach new audiences, particularly those who might be put off by productions not in their native tongue, and ensures that its work is as available as possible. This ethos is mirrored in the extraordinary access provided to the company's history by the Sophie Hamilton Archive (http://archive.cheekbyjowl.com/), which offers digitized copies of show reports, programmes, images, promptbooks and other invaluable material freely online. In opening up both its present and its future, Cheek by Jowl continues to pioneer.

The spirit of Cheek by Jowl is freedom; freedom for the actor, freedom for the tour, freedom for the art. The company office is a tiny but welcoming two-room cupboard at the Barbican Centre; the company's creative hub is wherever Donnellan and Ormerod happen to be. Like their productions, Cheek by Jowl is stripped down to what matters, giving all of its collaborators the freedom to innovate and challenge in the pursuit of a uniquely theatrical experience that comes alive in the space. For Shakespeare, as this book has shown, the consequences are radical and revitalizing, the plays treated as new work rather than revivals, with each moment in the text rediscovered in the live negotiations of bodies and space. The company's homepage offers a motto drawn from *The Actor and the Target* that epitomizes Cheek by Jowl's ethos: 'Theatre cannot die before the last dream has been dreamt' (Cheek by Jowl 2018b). Cheek by Jowl hasn't finished dreaming yet.

Appendix:
Cheek by Jowl
productions

This appendix lists all of Cheek by Jowl's productions up to 2018. Select other productions related to early modern drama directed by Donnellan and Ormerod away from Cheek by Jowl are marked in square brackets.

* = Chekhov International Theatre Festival in association with Cheek by Jowl.

** = Théâtre des Bouffes du Nord in association with Cheek by Jowl.

Years	Play	Language
[1980]	'Tis Pity She's a Whore [Theatre Space]	[English]
1981	The Country Wife	English
1982–3	Othello	English
1983–5	Vanity Fair	English
1984–5	Pericles	English
1984–5	Andromache	English
1985–6	A Midsummer Night's Dream	English
1985–6	The Man of Mode	English
1986–7	Twelfth Night	English
1986–7	The Cid	English
[1986]	Romeo and Juliet [New Shakespeare Company]	[English]
1987–8	Macbeth	English
1988	Family Affair	English

1988–9	*The Tempest*	English
1988–9	*Philoctetes*	English
1989	*The Doctor of Honour* [dir. Lindsay Posner]	English
1989	*Lady Betty*	English
1990	*Sara*	English
1990–1	*Hamlet*	English
1991–2	*As You Like It*	English
1993	*Don't Fool with Love/The Blind Men*	English
1994	*Measure for Measure*	English
1994–5	*As You Like It* (revival)	English
1995–6	*The Duchess of Malfi*	English
1997	*Out Cry* [dir. Timothy Walker]	English
[1997–]	*The Winter's Tale* [Maly Theatre]	[Russian]
1998	*Much Ado about Nothing*	English
2000–	*Boris Godunov* *	Russian
[2001]	*Falstaff* [Salzburg Festival]	[Italian]
2001–2	*Homebody/Kabul*	English
[2002]	*King Lear* [RSC Academy]	[English]
2003–14	*Twelfth Night* *	Russian
[2004]	*Romeo and Juliet* [Bolshoi Ballet]	[Russian]
2004	*Othello*	English
2005–	*Three Sisters* *	Russian
2006	*The Changeling*	English
2007	*Cymbeline*	English
2007–9	*Andromaque* **	French
2008	*Troilus and Cressida*	English
2009–11	*Macbeth*	English
2011–	*The Tempest*	Russian
2011–12	*'Tis Pity She's a Whore*	English
2012–13	*'Tis Pity She's a Whore* (revival)	English
2013–15	*Ubu Roi*	French
2013–	*Measure for Measure*	Russian
2014	*'Tis Pity She's a Whore* (revival)	English

[2015]	*Hamlet* [Bolshoi Ballet]	[Russian]
2016–17	*The Winter's Tale*	English
2016–	*Twelfth Night* (revival)	Russian
2018–19	*Périclès, Prince de Tyr*	French
[2018]	*The Revenger's Tragedy* [Piccolo Teatro]	[Italian]
2019–	*The Knight of the Burning Pestle*	Russian

NOTES

Introduction

1 At the time of writing, Donnellan and Ormerod are preparing to direct their first production in Italian, *The Revenger's Tragedy* (2018).

2 The move to be lead producer on the Russian and French work is relatively recent – *Andromaque*, for instance, was a Bouffes du Nord production that Cheek by Jowl effectively 'presented' in the UK, leading to the company's choice to produce in French for themselves (Byrne 2016).

3 Paul Menzer (2017: 101) notes the influence of Cheek by Jowl on the work of the American Shakespeare Center.

4 Others include multiple Olivier Awards, the Moscow Golden Mask Award and the honour of Chevalier de l'Ordre des Arts et des Lettres. Both Ormerod and Donnellan were awarded OBEs in 2017.

5 On integrated casting, see Rutter (2005: 346). See also the company page on the British Black and Asian Shakespeare website: https://bbashakespeare.warwick.ac.uk/organisations/cheek-jowl.

6 On *The Changeling*, see Solga (2009: 159–75).

7 In 1985, for *A Midsummer Night's Dream*, Cheek by Jowl began its tradition of a full company photo in its programmes, including directors, cast, creatives, technical team and administrators (Cheek by Jowl 1985).

8 Paddy Cunneen describes his 'Associate Director' status as 'a recognition of the proximity that they have in the rehearsal room rather than an appointment to an official position' (Reade 1991: 18).

9 Notably, in Maria M. Delgado and Paul Heritage's collection of interviews, Donnellan and Ormerod are the only pair interviewed (Donnellan and Ormerod 1996).

10 The company's archives have recently been made much more extensively available through the generous bequest of Sophie Hamilton, allowing the company to create an open access online archive: http://archive.cheekbyjowl.com.

11 Donnellan carries several other adapting credits, including for *Vanity Fair* and the librettos of *Romeo and Juliet* and *Hamlet* for the Bolshoi.

12 The interruption was occasioned by the sad passing of Alexei Dadonov, the original production's Olivia.

13 To date, Donnellan and Ormerod's screen credits include a short film, the self-penned *The Big Fish* (1992), which Simon Reade (1991: 117) notes draws on a childhood experience of Donnellan, and the starry feature film *Bel Ami* (2012), a choice perhaps reminiscent of their selection of *Vanity Fair* (1983–5) as one of Cheek by Jowl's first productions.

Chapter 1

1 Notes on the Russian production are taken from an undated archival recording made in 1997 at the Maly Theatre, courtesy of Cheek by Jowl.

2 Cunneen also contributed incidental music for *Ubu Roi* (2013–15).

3 In the event, two actors from the original run – Abubakar Salim (Camillo) and Chris Gordon (Florizel) – were unable to return to the company for the second run.

4 Rehearsals took place at the Jerwood Space in London in December 2016, and the detail from this chapter is taken from my own notes.

5 A typical example I observed was Donnellan and James agreeing to substitute 'with justice' for 'in justice' in 2.3.178–9, 'I do in justice charge thee, / On thy soul's peril.'

6 Speaking during the hiatus between the two runs, Radmall-Quirke offered a more detailed consideration. 'She's been in jail; I think she's had a little while to think about what she's going to say. The structures of thought in the first speech are so long and twisted and weird, convoluted – she's clearly over-thought what

she's going to say – that's my take on it. And then it gets more malicious and more direct, and the thoughts become much shorter as the trial progresses, and I think then she's riffing' (2016).

7 Most prominently, Antony Sher writes extensively about his consultations with psychiatrists of various specialisms in an attempt to 'diagnose [Leontes's] case' ahead of the RSC's 1999 production (Sher 1999).

Chapter 2

1 Production notes are taken from the archival recording made on 10 April 2011 at Brooklyn Academy of Music.

2 Detail of the production is taken from the archive video at the V&A, recorded on 23 January 1996 at Wyndham's Theatre.

3 An undated letter in the Cheek by Jowl archive remarks, 'Your company's short visit in Malta, during which you gave three performances much appreciated by the theatre-loving public and partially spoilt by a small pack of bigoted bullies, created a dose of healthy debate and controversy. Fortunately much of this revolved around alternative ways of looking at and doing theatre in contemporary society' (Cheek by Jowl 1996). The company chose not to engage in the public debate.

Chapter 3

1 Shakespeare's Globe's first all-male production was of *Henry V* in its 'Opening Season' (Carson and Karim-Cooper 2008: 239).

2 My notes are based on several viewings of the production in 2006 at Warwick Arts Centre and in 2007 at the Swan Theatre, Stratford-upon-Avon, and checked via the archival recording made at the Swan on 2 March 2007. *Pace* Thomas, I did not observe Kuzichev giggle, and Donnellan confirms he never did (2018).

3 Quotations in this section, including this adaptation of Sebastian's line, are taken from the final draft of the surtitle translation (Cheek by Jowl 2007a), kindly provided by the company. I refer to the cast members on this tour, though there have been several recastings over the years.

4 See also the naïve Miranda in *The Tempest*, the imprisoned Pompey in *Measure for Measure* and the ill Pericles in *Périclès*.

5 For a recent example, see the added rape scene in Rupert Goold's 2016 *Richard III*.

6 The other was *'Tis Pity She's a Whore*, which went through three cast changes across the 2011–12, 2012–13 and 2014 runs.

7 My comments on this production are based on an archival recording of the matinee of the 11 February 1995 performance at the Albery Theatre (now the Noel Coward), London, featuring the 1994–5 revival cast.

8 Lester notes that the Celias from the two runs were different in certain pertinent respects:

> Tom [Hollander] found a lot of humour in Celia. She was kind, loving but quietly very spoilt. Simon Coates built on that by finding an unloved pain to Celia. Both Celias felt a little bit betrayed when Rosalind fell in love. They got angry about it. Celia's line 'Oh wonderful, wonderful, and most wonderful, wonderful and yet again wonderful, and after that, out of all hooping' can look on the surface like she's pleased for Rosalind. Very, very happy. But at this point she hasn't told Rosalind who has written the poems and Rose is beside herself wanting to know who. With this in mind the actors found a slower delivery that had the audience in stitches as they recognised Celia's pointed sarcasm. (2016)

9 Bulman and others read the relationship as homoerotic; while this reading is certainly available, Lester felt that this was not about homosexuality, but about 'our girls' club – we grew up together, we were schooled together' (2016).

10 See the British Black and Asian Shakespeare Database: https://bbashakespeare.warwick.ac.uk/roles/Rosalind (accessed 21 April 2018).

Chapter 4

1 Both numbers are rough counts. The line count of *Cymbeline* is
   taken from Wayne (2017). The line count for Cheek by Jowl's
   production is a rough number based on a detailed analysis
   of the promptbook (Cheek by Jowl 2007b) and the archival
   recording made on 12 May 2007 at Brooklyn Academy of
   Music, which differs somewhat, notably in the reintroduction
   of lines omitted from the rehearsal text. Further, the lineation
   of the Cheek by Jowl script (itself adapted from the MIT free
   online version at http://shakespeare.mit.edu/cymbeline/full.html)
   differs significantly from Wayne in, for instance, the separation
   of half-lines of verse. Finally, the figures for the Cheek by Jowl
   text include a small number of newly written lines. However, the
   numbers give a fair estimate of the relative proportions of each
   scene retained for the production.

2 See notably *'Tis Pity She's a Whore* (2011–14), which cut the
   character of Bergetto and his subplot entirely (see Chapter 5).

3 The reproduced text is based on the promptbook, which
   represents the text being played by the final performance. In
   cross-referencing this with the archive recording, I use italics
   for text present only in the recording and strike-through for
   text present only in the promptbook. For convenience, I have
   added the names of the characters played by the named actors in
   square brackets.

4 Prescott notes the 'intriguing' nature of Cheek by Jowl
   promptbooks, which rather resist definition as such. As he notes,
   'the annotation of blocking and stage action is sparse, bordering
   on the gnomic' (2008: 73), a result both of Cheek by Jowl's
   relative economy of staging and the recurring presence of both
   Donnellan and Ormerod on tour.

5 Notes on this production are drawn from my own viewings of
   the production, confirmed by an undated archive video filmed at
   Les Geméaux in January or February 2011.

6 Ilyin was credited as 'Ilya Iliin' in the tour programme (Cheek by
   Jowl 2011a). The transliteration of Russian names into English
   can lead to several viable alternatives; I have standardized all
   names to a single spelling throughout this book.

7 Line references are from the Arden Shakespeare. Quotations are taken directly from the surtitles of the English tour (Cheek by Jowl 2011b), kindly provided by Cheek by Jowl.

8 The show reports for this performance only make mention that 'Freedom got huge applause' (Cheek by Jowl 1989d).

Chapter 5

1 This is a revision of a quotation that first appeared in Donnellan (1999: 21).

2 Notably, Ormerod designed Cheek by Jowl's *Out Cry* (1997), directed by Timothy Walker. Donnellan has only worked without Ormerod once, on *Le Cid* for the Avignon Festival (1998).

3 This is a revision of a quotation that first appeared in Ormerod (2002: 3).

4 Under Beth Byrne's executive directorship, the company renegotiated the terms of its Arts Council subsidy to remove a minimum number of domestic performances, thus freeing the company to serve the world (Byrne 2016).

5 The archive video records the 8 March 2012 performance at the Silk Street Theatre, Barbican.

6 Act and Scene numbers are taken from this edition.

7 The initial work on the dinner party took place in August 2012, before rehearsals resumed in November (Leterme 2016).

8 Xavier Boiffier (2016) notes the reception that the production received in Romania, in light of resonances drawn with the 'painful history' of the Ceauşescu period.

Chapter 6

1 Several critics at the time referred to it as Cheek by Jowl's final production (e.g. Butler 1998; Smallwood 1999).

2 According to 'Concordance', *Open Source Shakespeare*, https://www.opensourceshakespeare.org/concordance/findform.php (accessed 22 April 2018).

3 Notes on the production are taken from the archival recording made on 16 July 1998 at the Playhouse Theatre.

4 This is a revision of a quotation that first appeared in Ormerod (2002: 7).

5 This is a revision of a quotation that first appeared in Donnellan (2003: 166).

6 As Aleks Sierz notes, the company's 1994 *Measure for Measure* similarly kept Claudio 'on stage, imprisoned, so the audience can never forget that his life is at stake' (2010: 147).

7 Notes on this production are primarily based on the live-streamed performance broadcast on 22 April 2015 from the Barbican, London.

8 This is a revision of a quotation from Donnellan (2016).

9 The 'predicament' is central to Donnellan's forthcoming book, *The Carnal Space*.

REFERENCES

Quotations from early modern plays are taken from the third series of the Arden Shakespeare and the Arden Early Modern Drama single volumes, except where stated.

Aebischer, Pascale (2013), *Screening Early Modern Drama*, Cambridge: Cambridge University Press.

Aebischer, Pascale (2017), '*The Winter's Tale* presented by Cheek by Jowl', *Shakespeare Bulletin*, 35 (4): 721–5.

Aebischer, Pascale (forthcoming), *Shakespeare and the Technologies of Performance*, Cambridge: Cambridge University Press.

Anderson, Susan L. (2018), *Echo and Meaning on Early Modern English Stages*, Basingstoke: Palgrave Macmillan.

Baker, Edward (2016), 'Declan Donnellan to be Awarded the Golden Lion Award for Lifetime Achievement', *Broadway World*, 25 July. https://www.broadwayworld.com/westend/article/Declan-Donnellan-To-Be-Awarded-The-Golden-Lion-Award-For-Lifetime-Achievement-20160725 (accessed 22 April 2018).

Barker, Roberta (2007), *Early Modern Tragedy, Gender and Performance, 1984–2000*, Basingstoke: Palgrave Macmillan.

Barker, Roberta (2011), 'The Duchess High and Low: A Performance History of *The Duchess of Malfi*', in Christina Luckyj (ed.), *The Duchess of Malfi: A Critical Guide*, 42–65, London: Continuum.

Barker, Roberta, Kim Solga and Cary Mazer (2013), ''Tis Pity She's a Realist: A Conversational Case Study in Realism and Early Modern Theater Today', *Shakespeare Bulletin*, 31 (4): 571–97.

Barton, Anne (1986), 'Shakespeare's Sense of an Ending in *Twelfth Night*', in Stanley Wells (ed.), *Twelfth Night: Critical Essays*, 303–10, New York: Garland.

Berry, Ralph (1989), *On Directing Shakespeare*, London: Hamish Hamilton.

Billington, Michael (1991), 'Review of *As You Like It*', *Times*, 14 October.

Billington, Michael (2010), 'Macbeth (review)', *Guardian*, 25 March.

Billington, Michael (2013), 'Ubu Roi – review', *Guardian*, 12 April.

Billington, Michael (2017), 'Romeo and Juliet review – the Globe's perverse show vandalises Shakespeare', *Guardian*, 28 April.

Birksted-Breen, Noah (2016), 'Review of Shakespeare's *Measure for Measure*', *Shakespeare*, 12 (1): 88–91.

Boiffier, Xavier (2016), interview with the author, 30 September.

Boon, Maxim (2017), '*Measure for Measure* (Cheek by Jowl, Pushkin Theatre Moscow)', *The Music*, 8 January. http://themusic.com.au/arts/reviews/2017/01/11/measure-for-measure-review-cheek-by-jowl-pushkin-theatre-moscow-maxim-boon/ (accessed 22 April 2018).

Bordwell, David and Kristin Thompson (2015), *Film Art: An Introduction*, 10th edn, New York: McGraw-Hill.

Brantley, Ben (1995), 'Theatre Review; A "Duchess" Returns, Engulfed by Depravity', *New York Times*, 1 December.

Brantley, Ben (1998), 'Theatre Review: Lovers Still Bickering, in War and Peace', *New York Times*, 30 March.

Brantley, Ben (2009), 'Of Czars and Blood, Ambition and Power', *New York Times*, 23 July.

Brantley, Ben (2012), 'Delivering Verse in Naughty Positions', *New York Times*, 23 March.

Brown, J.P.C. (2014), 'Seeing Double: Dramaturgy and the Experience of *Twelfth Night*', *Shakespeare*, 10 (3): 293–308.

Bulman, James C. (2008), 'Bringing Cheek by Jowl's *As You Like It* Out of the Closet: The Politics of Queer Theater', in James C. Bulman (ed.), *Shakespeare Re-Dressed*, 79–95, Cranbury, NJ: Fairleigh Dickinson University Press.

Butler, Robert (1998), 'There's Much Ado and it's All in Perfect Order', *Independent*, 13 June.

Byrne, Beth (2016), interview with the author, 22 January.

Cabra, Fausto (2018), email to the author, 3 May.

Carson, Christie and Farah Karim-Cooper, eds (2008), *Shakespeare's Globe: A Theatrical Experiment*, Cambridge: Cambridge University Press.

Cavendish, Dominic (1998), '*Much Ado about Nothing* (review)', *Time Out*, 10 June.

Cavendish, Dominic (2012), '*'Tis Pity She's a Whore*, Cheek by Jowl, Barbican, review', *Telegraph*, 22 February.

Cavendish, Dominic (2015a), '*Measure for Measure*, Cheek by Jowl, Barbican: "like a punch to the guts"', *Telegraph*, 17 April.

Cavendish, Dominic (2015b), 'Ubu Roi: An Unforgiving Satire on Manners Old and Modern', Telegraph, 20 July.

Cheek by Jowl (1983), Vanity Fair show reports, 21 November–3 December. Cheek by Jowl archives, V&A, THM 24/2/2.

Cheek by Jowl (1985), A Midsummer Night's Dream, programme, Sophie Hamilton Archive. http://archive.cheekbyjowl.com/ wp-content/uploads/2015/02/1985-MSNDpdf.compressed.pdf (accessed 22 April 2018).

Cheek by Jowl (1989a), publicity blurb for Lady Betty by Sharon Kean. Cheek by Jowl archives, V&A, THM 24/2/10.

Cheek by Jowl (1989b), Cheek by Jowl marketing material. Cheek by Jowl archives, V&A, THM 24/2/10.

Cheek by Jowl (1989c), fax from Barbara Matthews to Elizabeth Cardosa, 24 January. Cheek by Jowl archives, V&A, THM 24/2/8.

Cheek by Jowl (1989d), show report for The Tempest, 23 March. Cheek by Jowl archives, V&A, THM 24/2/8.

Cheek by Jowl (1991a), 'History, Policies and Role', Cheek by Jowl Archives, V&A, THM 24/1/1.

Cheek by Jowl (1991b), show reports from Farnham (24 July) and Bury St Edmunds (10 September). Cheek by Jowl Archives, V&A, THM 24/2/13.

Cheek by Jowl (1994a), letter from the British Council in Bulgaria, 9 December. Cheek by Jowl Archives, V&A, THM 24/2/16.

Cheek by Jowl (1994b), As You Like It welcome pack. Cheek by Jowl Archives, V&A, THM 24/2/16.

Cheek by Jowl (1995a), 'Review of Cheek by Jowl's board retreat, 12 August 1995', minutes by Nicola Thorold. Cheek by Jowl Archives, V&A, THM 24/1/1.

Cheek by Jowl (1995b), 'Assistant Administrator Handbook'. Cheek by Jowl Archives, V&A, THM 24/1/2.

Cheek by Jowl (1996), undated letter from Lino Sant to the company. Cheek by Jowl Archives, V&A, THM 24/2/17.

Cheek by Jowl (1998), Much Ado about Nothing rehearsal notes by Mike Draper, 9 January, Sophie Hamilton Archive. http://archive. cheekbyjowl.com/wp-content/uploads/2014/11/MUCH_ADO_ REHNOTES.pdf (accessed 22 April 2018).

Cheek by Jowl (2007a), Twelfth Night UK tour surtitles, 2006–7.

Cheek by Jowl (2007b), Cymbeline promptbook, Sophie Hamilton Archive. http://archive.cheekbyjowl.com/

wp-content/uploads/2014/12/CYMBELINE-PROMPT-SCRIPT11092014153311_01.pdf (accessed 22 April 2018).

Cheek by Jowl (2007c), *Three Sisters* programme, Sophie Hamilton Archive. http://archive.cheekbyjowl.com/wp-content/uploads/2014/12/Three-Sisters_Pgs-with-kremlin.pdf (accessed 22 April 2018).

Cheek by Jowl (2011a), *The Tempest* programme.

Cheek by Jowl (2011b), *The Tempest* UK tour surtitles, 2006–7.

Cheek by Jowl (2016), email to Cheek by Jowl mailing list, 28 June.

Cheek by Jowl (2018a), 'People', *Cheek by Jowl*. http://www.cheekbyjowl.com/people.php (accessed 22 April 2018).

Cheek by Jowl (2018b), 'Home', *Cheek by Jowl*. http://www.cheekbyjowl.com (accessed 22 April 2018).

Collins, Eleanor (2010), '*Macbeth* (review)', *Cahiers Élisabéthains*, 78: 63–5.

Collins, Eleanor (2012), 'Review of *The Tempest*', *Shakespeare*, 8 (1): 96–9.

Collins, Eleanor and Peter J. Smith (2013), 'Review of John Ford's '*Tis Pity She's a Whore*', *Shakespeare*, 9 (2): 248–51.

Coveney, Michael (2006), 'The Changeling, Barbican, London', *Independent*, 16 May.

Cox, John F., ed. (1997), *Much Ado about Nothing*, Cambridge: Cambridge University Press.

Curtis, Nick (1994), 'How We Met: Declan Donnellan and Nick Ormerod', *Independent*, 16 January.

Donnellan, Declan (1989), *Lady Betty*, Sophie Hamilton Archive. http://archive.cheekbyjowl.com/wp-content/uploads/2014/12/Lady-Betty-script.pdf (accessed 22 April 2018).

Donnellan, Declan (1999), 'Declan Donnellan', in Gabriella Giannachi and Mark Luckhurst (eds), *On Directing: Interviews with Directors*, 19–23, London: Faber and Faber.

Donnellan, Declan (2003), 'Directing Shakespeare's Comedies: In Conversation with Peter Holland', *Shakespeare Survey*, 56: 161–6.

Donnellan, Declan (2005), *The Actor and the Target*, revised edn, London: Nick Hern.

Donnellan, Declan (2009), 'Declan Donnellan (b.1953)', in Maria Shevtsova and Christopher Innes (eds), *Directors/Directing: Conversations on Theatre*, 66–91, Cambridge: Cambridge University Press.

Donnellan, Declan (2014), 'All you need is love: Adrian Lester and the miraculous all-male *As You Like It*', *Guardian*, 12 November.

Donnellan, Declan (2016), 'Golden Lion Awards speech 29 July', *YouTube*, 17 August. https://www.youtube.com/watch?v=Sv-61MFhlys (accessed 22 April 2018).

Donnellan, Declan (2018), email to the author, 27 April.

Donnellan, Declan and Nick Ormerod (1996), 'Declan Donnellan and Nick Ormerod', in Maria M. Delgado and Paul Heritage (eds), *In Contact with the Gods?: Directors Talk Theatre*, 79–92, Manchester: Manchester University Press.

Donnellan, Declan and Nick Ormerod (2015), pre-show interview, *Ubu Roi* live broadcast, 26 July.

Donnellan, Declan and Nick Ormerod (2016), interview with the author, 14 September.

Drew, William (2015), '*Measure for Measure*', *Exeunt*, 21 April. http://exeuntmagazine.com/reviews/measure-for-measure-2/ (accessed 22 April 2018).

Dunnett, Roderic (2013), '*Ubu Roi*', *Exeunt*, 4 February. http://exeuntmagazine.com/reviews/ubu-roi/ (accessed 22 April 2018).

Edmondson, Paul (2007), '*Twelfth Night, or What You Will*', *Cahiers Élisabéthains*, special issue: 80–2.

Feklistov, Alexander (2016), email to the author, trans. Anya Kolesnikova, 6 December.

Fernandez, Imma (2013), 'Venice surrenders to Donnellan's frenzied "*Ubu Roi*"', trans. Cheek by Jowl, *El Periodico*, 6 August. http://www.cheekbyjowl.com/media/press/uburoi_el_periodico_06082013.pdf (accessed 22 April 2018).

Gay, Penny (1994), *As She Likes It: Shakespeare's Unruly Women*, London: Taylor & Francis.

Gibson, Jane (2016), interview with the author, 28 January.

Goodland, Katherine (2007), '*Cymbeline* presented by Cheek by Jowl', *Shakespeare Bulletin*, 25 (4): 135–41.

Greenwood, Judith, ed. (1998), *Cheek by Jowl Education Pack*.

Greenwood, Judith (2016), interview with the author, 3 March.

Hemming, Sarah (1991), 'Taking it Like a Man', *Independent*, 20 November.

Hille, Anastasia (2016), interview with the author, 18 October.

Holland, Peter (1992), 'Shakespeare Performances in England 1990–1', *Shakespeare Survey*, 45: 115–44.

Holland, Peter (2012), 'Openings', in Stuart Hampton-Reeves and
    Bridget Escolme (eds), *Shakespeare and the Making of Theatre*,
    14–31, Basingstoke: Palgrave Macmillan.

Holmes, Jonathan (2012), 'Adrian Lester', in John Russell Brown
    (ed.), *The Routledge Companion to Actors' Shakespeare*, 132–42,
    London: Routledge.

Horsley, Owen (2016), interview with the author, 12 February.

Huet, Stéphane (2012), "*'Tis Pity She's a Whore* (review)', *Cahiers
    Élisabéthains*, 81: 75–7.

Innes, Christopher and Maria Shevtsova (2013), *The Cambridge
    Introduction to Theatre Directing*, Cambridge: Cambridge
    University Press.

Isherwood, Charles (2007), 'Confusion and Deception as a Royal
    Family Affair', *New York Times*, 12 May.

Isherwood, Charles (2011), 'Ambition Doth Curse All Makes of
    Men', *New York Times*, 6 April.

James, Orlando (2016), interview with the author, 19 May.

Johnson, Nora (1998), 'Ganymedes and Kings: Staging Male
    Homosexual Desire in *The Winter's Tale*', *Shakespeare Studies*,
    26: 187–217.

Kamaralli, Anna (2012), *Shakespeare and the Shrew*, Basingstoke:
    Palgrave Macmillan.

Keith, Beverly and G. Legman, trans. (2003), *Ubu Roi*, Mineola, NY:
    Dover Thrift.

Khalilulina, Anna (2017), email to the author, trans. Anya
    Kolesnikova, 10 May.

Kirwan, Peter (2017), 'Not-Shakespeare and the Shakespearean
    Ghost', in James C. Bulman (ed.), *The Oxford Handbook
    of Shakespeare and Performance*, 87–103, Oxford: Oxford
    University Press.

Kirwan, Peter (2018), 'Cheek by Jowl: Reframing Complicity in
    Web-Streams of *Measure for Measure*', in Pascale Aebischer,
    Suzanne Greenhalgh and Laurie E. Osborne (eds), *Shakespeare
    and the 'Live' Theatre Broadcast Experience*, 161–73, London:
    Bloomsbury.

Kolesnikova, Anya (2016), interview with the author, 20 September.

Lang, Eleanor (2017), interview with the author, 14 February.

Lester, Adrian (2016), interview with the author, 20 March.

Leterme, Cécile (2016), interview with the author, 29 September.

Letts, Quentin (2018), 'Lusty revival has two waggy stars', *Daily
    Mail*, 6 April.

Lindley, David, ed. (2013), *The Tempest*, revised edn, Cambridge: Cambridge University Press.

Logan, Brian (1998), 'Okey Blokey', *Observer*, 14 June.

Macfadyen, Matthew (2016), interview with the author, 19 April.

Marlowe, Sam (2017), 'Theatre: *The Winter's Tale* at the Barbican', *Times*, 11 April.

Marshall, Cynthia, ed. (2004), *As You Like It*, Cambridge: Cambridge University Press.

Matthews, Barbara (2016), interview with the author, 19 March.

Mazer, Cary M. (2008), 'Rosalind's Breast', in James C. Bulman (ed.), *Shakespeare Re-Dressed*, 96–115, Cranbury, NJ: Fairleigh Dickinson University Press.

McEachern, Claire, ed. (2016), *Much Ado about Nothing*, revised edn, London: Bloomsbury.

McNulty, Charles (2013), 'Theater review: "*'Tis Pity*" still shocks after nearly 400 years', *LA Times*, 11 January.

Mentz, Steve (2011), '*Macbeth* (review)', *Shakespeare Bulletin*, 29 (4): 621–6.

Mentz, Steve (2012), '*'Tis Pity She's a Whore* (review)', *Shakespeare Bulletin*, 30 (3): 322–4.

Menzer, Paul (2017), *Shakespeare in the Theatre: The American Shakespeare Center*, London: Bloomsbury.

Moreton, Peter (2016), interview with the author, 19 May.

Nathan, David (1998), '*Much Ado about Nothing* (review)', *Jewish Chronicle*, 12 June.

Ormerod, Nick (2002), 'Designing Shakespeare', Sophie Hamilton Archive, 16 December. http://archive.cheekbyjowl.com/wp-content/uploads/2015/03/DS_NO-TRANSCRIPT1.pdf (accessed 22 April 2018).

Ormerod, Nick (2009), 'Making a Scene: the World of Theatre Design', *Guardian*, 12 November. https://www.theguardian.com/stage/theatreblog/2009/nov/12/theatre-design-linbury-prize (accessed 22 April 2018).

Ormerod, Nick (2016), '"Tom Hiddleston sang a boyband number": Nick Ormerod on *Cymbeline*', *Guardian*, 1 August.

Palfrey, Simon and Tiffany Stern (2007), *Shakespeare in Parts*, Oxford: Oxford University Press.

Peter, John (1991), 'Review of *As You Like It*', *Sunday Times*, 8 December.

Power, Terri (2016), *Shakespeare and Gender in Practice*, Basingstoke: Palgrave Macmillan.

Prescott, Paul (2008), 'Declan Donnellan', in John Russell Brown
    (ed.), *The Routledge Companion to Directors' Shakespeare*,
    69–85, London: Routledge.
Purcell, Stephen (2016), 'Shakespeare Performances in England (and
    Wales), 2015', *Shakespeare Survey*, 69: 394–431.
Purcell, Stephen (2017), *Shakespeare in the Theatre: Mark Rylance
    at the Globe*, London: Bloomsbury.
Radmall-Quirke, Natalie (2016), interview with the author, 19 May.
Rank, Julia (2012), ''Tis Pity She's a Whore', *Exeunt*, 23 February.
    http://exeuntmagazine.com/reviews/tis-pity-shes-a-whore/
    (accessed 22 April 2018).
Reade, Simon (1991), *Cheek by Jowl: Ten Years of Celebration*,
    Bath: Absolute.
Reeves, Saskia (2003), *Actors on Shakespeare: Much Ado about
    Nothing*, London: Faber and Faber.
Reid, Christina (1989), *Two Plays*, London: Methuen.
Remshardt, Ralf (2004), *Staging the Savage God*, Carbondale:
    Southern Illinois University Press.
Richardson, Joy (2016), interview with the author, 19 March.
Rutter, Carol Chillington (2005), 'Maverick Shakespeare' in Barbara
    Hodgdon and W.B. Worthen (eds), *A Companion to Shakespeare
    and Performance*, 335–58, Malden, MA: Blackwell.
Rutter, Carol Chillington (2011), 'Shakespeare Performances in
    England 2010', *Shakespeare Survey*, 64: 340–77.
Rutter, Carol Chillington (2012), 'Shakespeare Performances in
    England (and Wales) 2011', *Shakespeare Survey*, 65: 445–83.
Shapiro, James (2016), email to the author, 27 October.
Shaughnessy, Robert (2017), *As You Like It*, Manchester:
    Manchester University Press.
Sher, Antony (1999), 'Arts: How I Got Into the Mad Bard's Head',
    Guardian, 2 January. https://www.theguardian.com/books/1999/
    jan/02/books.guardianreview5 (accessed 22 April 2018).
Shevtsova, Maria (2005), 'Declan Donnellan (1953–)', in Shomit
    Miller and Maria Shevtsova (eds), *Fifty Key Theatre Directors*,
    231–6, London: Routledge.
Shulman, Milton (1987), '*Macbeth* (review)', *London Evening
    Standard*, 17 November.
Sierz, Aleks (2010), 'Declan Donnellan and Cheek by Jowl', in Maria
    M. Delgado and Dan Rebellato (eds), *Contemporary European
    Theatre Directors*, 145–64, Abingdon: Routledge.

Silverstone, Catherine (2010), 'Fatal Attraction: Desire, Anatomy and Death in *'Tis Pity She's a Whore*', in Lisa Hopkins (ed.), *'Tis Pity She's a Whore: A Critical Guide*, 77–93, London: Bloomsbury.

Smallwood, Robert (1999), 'Shakespeare Performances in England, 1998', *Shakespeare Survey*, 52: 229–53.

Smith, Peter. J. (2007), 'Review of William Shakespeare's *Cymbeline*', *Shakespeare*, 3 (3): 352–5.

Solga, Kim (2009), *Violence Against Women in Early Modern Performance*, Basingstoke: Palgrave Macmillan.

Sullivan, Erin (2013), 'A Disease unto Death: Sadness in the Time of Shakespeare', in Elena Carrera (ed.), *Emotions and Health, 1200–1700*, 159–84, Leiden: Brill.

Taylor, Paul (1994), 'Theatre/Hollow men', *Independent*, 20 June.

Taylor, Paul (2013), 'Theatre review: *Ubu Roi*, Barbican, London', *Independent*, 12 April.

Thomas, Chad Allen (2010), 'On Queering *Twelfth Night*', *Theatre Topics*, 20 (2): 101–11.

Vallejo, Javier (2013), 'King Ubu: bourgeois, incisive and hilarious', trans. Cheek by Jowl, *El País Madrid Sábado*, 28 September. http://www.cheekbyjowl.com/media/press/uburoi_el_pai_madrid_sabado_28092013.pdf (accessed 22 April 2018).

Vela, Arantxa (2016), email to the author, 2 October.

Wayne, Valerie, ed. (2017), *Cymbeline*, London: Bloomsbury.

Wojciehowski, Hannah C., ed. (2015), *Cymbeline*, Indianapolis, IN: Hackett.

Yoshino, Kenji (2009), 'On Empathy in Judgment (*Measure for Measure*)', *Cleveland State Law Review*, 57: 683–701.

INDEX